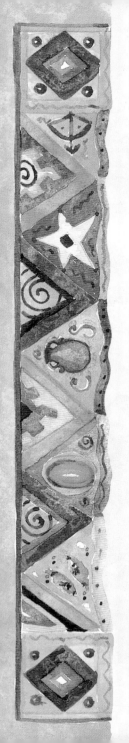

WHO AM I?

A key to your inner Nature and Personality

PAMELA ALLARDICE

ILLUSTRATED BY PENNY LOVELOCK

SMITHMARK

This edition published in 1999 by SMITHMARK Publishers,
a division of U.S. Media Holdings Inc.,
115 West 18th Street, New York, NY, 10011

SMITHMARK books are available for bulk purchase for sales promotion and premium use.
For details write or call the manager of special sales, SMITHMARK publishers,
115 West 18th Street, New York, NY, 10011.

First Published by Lansdowne Publishing Pty Ltd in 1994
Reprinted 1995

© Copyright design and illustration: Lansdowne Publishing Pty Ltd 1994

Publishing Manager: Deborah Nixon
Production Manager: Sally Stokes
Project Coordinator/Editor: Bronwyn Hilton
Designer: Kathie Baxter Smith
Formatted in 10.5pt MPerpetua on Quark Xpress

Produced by Phoenix Offset, Hong Kong

ISBN 0-7651-1683-9

Printed in China

Library of Congress Catalog Card Number: 99-70871

Contents

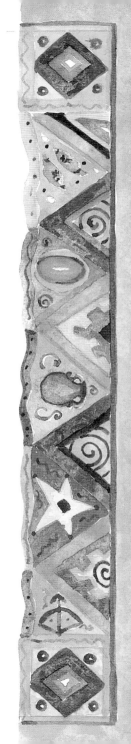

Introduction

SELF-KNOWLEDGE IS A wonderous thing. Know thyself, declared the Oracle at Delphi when the Ancient Greeks sought advice for future happiness. Since time immemorial, people have looked to the heavens for enlightenment. Some have sought to penetrate the mysteries of life through numerology, the study of numbers. The wise ones linked astrology and numerology with meaning they drew from the earth itself: its colors, its herbs and flowers, its gemstones.

This book is a clear and comprehensive repository of this knowledge for all who pursue the continuing challenge to understand themselves and others in our wonderful, complicated and confusing modern world. This book invites you to take a warmly perceptive look at yourself and the people in your life: friends and lovers, husbands and wives, parents and children, brothers and sisters, business colleagues and neighbors.

Your inner nature and personality are revealed through analysis not only of the individual Star Sign designated by your month of birth but also by your Rising Sign, depending on your time of birth, be it Aries, Taurus, Gemini, Cancer, Leo, Virgo, Libra, Scoprio, Sagittarius, Capricorn, Aquarius or Pisces. These together give a more rounded astrological reading than either can alone.

Thus equipped perhaps you'll feel more confident about a steady relationship with, say, a quicksilver Gemini. And after reading this book you'll know to charm Gemini with the gift of a moonstone, lilies of the valley or a perfect rose; but to give a gorgeous garnet, holly or carnations to ... which sign? The legends behind birth stones and

birth flowers are treats in store for you in these pages.

Or, take that impatient friend of yours, the Aries who wears the special Arian color of red, has a birth number One and drives your deliberate Taurean self (birth number Eight) into a rage. After reading you'll understand that you two are bound to lock horns occasionally — and maybe you should call a truce over a nice cup of herbal tea brewed under the auspices of your ruling Planets: straight peppermint for Taurus, rosemary with lavender for Aries.

Readers will discover that the powers of the four basic elements are harnessed by the Stars of the Zodiac so that the Star Signs of Fire nurture creative spirits and those of the Air foster the intellect, while the Earth Signs form a cluster for the world's materialists and the Water Signs a harbor for the emotional ones among us.

Who can say what extra insights you might gain from the wisdom of the Orient which are presented here? Chinese astrology's 12 year cycle encompassing the Years of the Dragon, Snake, Horse, Sheep, Monkey, Rooster, Dog, Boar, Rat, Buffalo, Tiger and Rabbit offers another framework for understanding human nature in all its variety.

You, your friends and family — whoever delves into this volume — will both delight and profit from exploring the accumulated knowledge of centuries offered by this pleasurable guide to who each one of us is and why we are the way we are. Have fun.

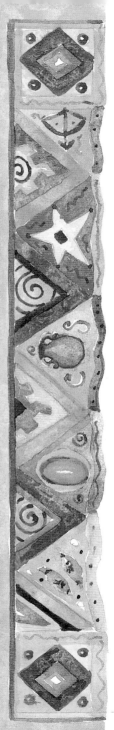

Zodiac Signs

 MUCH OF THE MODERN world's knowledge of the Zodiac comes to it via generations of gypsy lore which is also rich in herbal remedies for many of our human ailments. In gypsy culture, the Earth (de Develski) is the Divine Mother of all existence, the supreme deity for these people who live an outdoor life at one with Nature, who use a secret sign language sourced in their knowledge of leaves and grasses, and who can whistle the birds right out of the trees.

Gypsies believe that the Earth's abundant life forms throb to a shared life force, the power of the universe. They believe that, as planets other than our own whirl and pulsate in their courses, their rythym is at one with ours.

Nicolas Culpeper, England's seventeenth century herbalist and astrologer, shared this philosophy. He assigned each herb its ruling planet and dealt with each according to its Zodiac character be that impulsive Aries, restless Sagittarius or tenacious Scorpio. He wrote:

"Let the planet that governs the herb be angular and the stronger the better. If they can, in herbs of Saturn let Saturn be the ascendant; in the herbs of Mars, let Mars be in the mid-Heaven, for in those houses they delight. Let the Moon apply to them by good aspect and let her not be in the houses of her enemies."

As you stand on the threshold of discovering the wonderful world of astrology and its connection with ancient herbal remedies, modern researchers are discovering that various plants possess unique characteristics and emit energy in distinctive wave patterns and fields of force.

Most people already know where the Sun was in the traditional Zodiac chart when they were born. It's quite usual for someone to say 'I am an Aries' because their birthdate is between 22 March and 20 April which is when the Sun is in the ascendant.

It is because birth charts are so complicated and individual that they're so interesting. Your Zodiac birth chart is as distinctive as you are!

Aries

21 MARCH — 20 APRIL
RULING PLANET — MARS
SIGN — THE RAM
ELEMENT — FIRE

Key characteristics

FORCEFUL; A FIGHTER OR PIONEER. MAY DISPLAY AN INTEREST IN FIRE AND METAL.

> *The Ram having pass'd the Sea serenely shines,*
> *And leads the Year, the Prince of all the Signs.*
>
> *Manilius*

Temperament

Those born under Aries, particularly those born around 21 March, tend to be warm hearted as well as ambitious. Not only are they keen to seek opportunities for advancement, they are especially attracted to fresh, unexplored fields in which to seek their fortune. Those born under this Sign are on the Earth to discover things, and born with the energy, determination and resourcefulness to do so against all odds.

They are highly individualistic, sometimes quite topsy-turvy in their approach to life, but usually hardworking. Compromise does not come easily to them and they are impatient. They may also be quick tempered and sharp tongued.

Typically, Arians are involved in very positive and productive occupations that involve the laying of foundations or building in some way. Architecture, engineering, education, or philanthropic pursuits all fall within the ambit of the Arian disposition.

As Arian energy will probably reap material rewards and riches in early to middle life, it is Aries people who, often following their retirement from the world of business or professional practice, may guide the fortunes of benevolent institutions of many kinds. Older Arians may be found anywhere a great deal of helpful energy and work are required in return for little if any financial return.

They often excel at effective presentation and so make good salespeople — preferably of one product only because Arians are usually at their best when narrowing their focus.

Arians tend to be emotional as well as highly communicative and consequently may also do very well in the performing arts. Their strengths as communicators may mean that they have a talent for telepathy or clairvoyancy. Some may have the gift of prophecy, dreaming of events before they come to pass.

Preferring to 'go with the flow' and follow their instincts rather than stick to the facts, Arians are great ones for acting on hunches. Conversely, they don't usually shine at matters involving facts or figures, such as statistics or notetaking.

Love and friendship

Arians thrive in relationships with partners who help implement the Arian's ambitious plans and are towers of strength in tough times. But Arians are usually strong enough to survive any mismatch. More often than not, they will fulfil most of their potential, no matter what the nature of their personal or professional partnerships.

A quietly systematic partner who is patient and adaptable will help the fiery Aries in life. The ideal partner for those born under the Sign of the Ram is someone with a generous nature, able to overlook the odd slight or rudeness when their Arian is extremely brusque, for instance when intent on finishing a job.

Arians tend to ask a great deal of themselves, and of others. They like to give free rein to their energies and will be happiest amongst friends who aren't daunted by their ardent, sometimes forceful natures. Not everyone can keep up with a determined Aries!

Herbs and health

World leaders are frequently drawn from the Arian ranks. Outwardly confident, active and energetic, ambitious and curious Arians also can suffer from stress, often frustration. Not surprisingly, the head is the body part most often afflicted in Aries people. When their ceaseless daily activity gets too much even for energetic Arians, and their heads hurt from all that ram-like 'headbutting' or they're feeling distressed by life, then bring on the herbs ruled by the planets Mars (named for the Roman god of war) and Mercury (the winged messenger of Roman mythology): horseradish, marjoram, rosemary and garlic.

The elemental fire of horseradish is compatible with the Arian desire for fierce remedies and quick results. It can relieve their sinus troubles, and garlic will relieve asthmatic conditions. A simple, straightforward tea to please any Arian with a headache can be made by infusing a handful of sweet marjoram in boiling water.

Rosemary is the herb of memory, a traditional symbol of remembrance. In the words of Shakespeare's romantic Ophelia: There's rosemary, that's for remembrance; pray you, love, remember. Its very memorable aroma haunts many a fragrant potpourri blend of herbs and flowers. Its scent is said to improve memory and to promote a calm but alert state of mind. Just what an anxious or aggravated Arian needs!

They will experience the same pleasure when inhaling the pleasing aroma of a bath scented with rosemary sprigs. Added to shampoo, or to water as a hair rinse, rosemary will make hair gleam while its lingering perfume offers a continuing benefit to an Arian sense of wellbeing.

Rosemary combines well with lavender, infused as a tea and sweetened with honey. This makes a comforting bedtime drink for many Arians when they're struggling with feverish head colds.

Taurus

21 APRIL — 20 MAY
PLANET — VENUS
SIGN — THE BULL
ELEMENT — EARTH

Key characteristics

ARTISTIC, TASTEFUL, APPRECIATES BEAUTY. A LOVER OF HOME COMFORTS.
LOYAL. ROMANTIC.

Temperament

Like their namesake the Bull, Taureans are often handsome people although tending to be thickly set and heavier than others in stance and facial feature. If finely formed they, as well as their sturdier brothers and sisters under this Sun Sign, almost certainly will be blessed with exceptional mental and physical strength and fortitude. Overall stamina is a key characteristic of those born under the Sign of Taurus. These people can placidly work through very long hours when more mercurial temperaments would suffer mental, emotional and physical burnout.

Taurean workers are also trustworthy, determined, purposeful, systematic, detail oriented and highly productive. They enjoy routine and are not easily ruffled. They are the 'solid achiever' type.

Many Taureans have an excellent instinct for business and a naturally sound financial sense, but they are unlikely to be impressed by the accumulation of wealth for its own sake although they often build up quite substantial fortunes through hard work and diligence. Neither are they ambitious for ambition's sake, but they will pursue genuine advancement.

15

They enjoy all occupations that call for study, fine observation, accurate records or management skills. Taureans often become accountants or teachers. The Sign also boasts a fair representation of soldiers, lawyers, editors and navigators. Especially if born towards the latter third of the Sign, around 5 May, they may be highly creative. These Taureans will be drawn to a wide range of hands-on pursuits to express their creativity and love of beauty. Exceptional cooks, gardeners and embroiderers are often creative Taureans.

Taureans born early in the Sign period (around 21-23 April) may become frequent travellers either for business (perhaps as salespeople or importers) or for pleasure. But more often than not, Taureans prefer to stay close to hearth and home. They ask for nothing more than to enjoy a pleasant voyage through life. So neither do the intrigues of politics, either at home or in the workplace, appeal to Taureans.

Honest, straightforward and open handed (although not necessarily open minded!), Taureans make loyal and trusted friends themselves. But if betrayed, Taureans also can be trusted to turn vengeful, quickly and with devastating consequences for their enemies. They can also be very critical at times. If the mood takes them, they'll flex their stubborn streak and stand their ground over a small point rather than give an inch. And if Taureans don't understand something, false pride may lead them to disparage it as not worth knowing about.

Taureans without tempers are rare ones indeed, especially if born on or around 26 April. Many Taureans must fight their biggest battles with this aspect of their own temperaments if they are not to bring pain to themselves and others. Sometimes their negative potential surfaces as ruthlessness which Taurean providers justify as necessary for their legendary success. It's an understatement to say it's much better to have them on your side — with you rather than against you!

Love and friendship

With their partners, most Taureans are tender and supportive. Ideally, their partners should be similarly appreciative of the peace and beauty which Taureans almost invariably seek to create in their homes. Because Taureans are not usually very perspicacious, they will

do well to find partners who are. For instance, the right partner for a Taurean is one who can gently redirect a strong and stubborn character away from poor career choices to those where their talents will be realized and rewarded. Interestingly, Taureans may combine a partnership within a marriage or other personal relationship with a successful business or commercial endeavor.

Herbs and health

In their later years, Taureans may put on weight because while they love food, they loathe regular and energetic exercise. Combined with their tendency to bad temper, this means that many Taureans experience digestive problems. Herbal astrology teaches that such discomforts respond to plants ruled by Venus, the Taureans' ruling planet.

Among these herbs are the various mints, their famous, lively scents redolent of freshness and good health. A sprig of mint, steeped in a glass of water for a short time, then strained, makes a pleasant mouthwash and a cup of peppermint tea is a renowned carminative. An infusion of mint may help to sooth skin troubles reflecting Taurean indulgence in an excess of rich and sugary foods.

Tansy, both attractively bitter and aromatic, is another herb of Venus and renowned as a digestive aid. Tansy pudding was eaten at medieval feasts to counter the effects of over-eating.

Thyme is another Taurean herb. Any recipes using thyme should be beneficial to Taurean digestive systems as those born under this Sign take their habitual, everyday pleasure in eating and drinking.

In olden days, girls placed sprigs of thyme under their pillows to prevent nightmares. Twentieth-century Taureans should try the same remedy when they're tossing and turning in sleep.

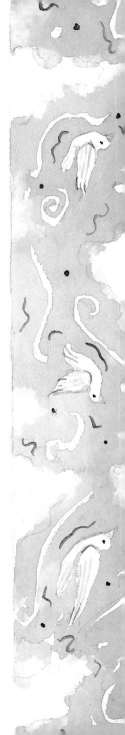

Gemini

21 MAY — 21 JUNE
PLANET — MERCURY
SIGN — THE TWINS
ELEMENT — AIR

Key characteristics

QUICK, CLEVER, VERSATILE, IMPATIENT. SELF-EXPRESSION IS A NECESSITY, NOT A LUXURY. CAN BE LITERARY OR MUSICAL.

Tender Gemini in strict embrace
Stand clos'd and smiling in each other's Face

Manilius

Temperament

People born under the Sign of the Twins usually can turn a hand to many different types of work and study. They enjoy the variety while others admire them as skilled yet carefree Jacks and Jills of all trades. Those born towards the beginning of the Sign, up until 27 May or thereabouts, are likely to be especially lucky in life, being blessed with a very wide-reaching mental capacity and a jovial nature.

Geminis seem to attract more than their fair share of good luck. Gypsy astrologers ask those born under Gemini to perform ceremonial tasks or undertake commercial projects on behalf of their tribes. Following their instincts, taking chances in business which often involves foreign interests, seems to bear fruit more often than not with this Sign.

Typically, Geminis have finely developed instincts for communicating with others and do so very effectively and entertainingly. They have a natural ability to talk.

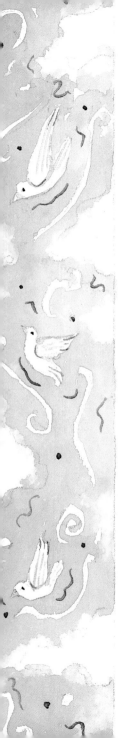

Their abundance of optimistic and positive energy may mean that a career in sales will appeal to them, along with more classically creative endeavors, such as music and the visual arts. Involvements with design, decorating or color related projects are all favored. Many Geminis have a strong sense of aesthetics.

Geminis also do well professionally within the world of print or electronic media. In particular, photography, journalism or other work in newspapers, magazines and television seems well suited to them.

It is quite usual for Geminis to have more than one career, sometimes simultaneously! They also may be found working and studying at the same time. Such study may be a hobby, a healthy outlet for excess Gemini energy and ability.

It is also quite usual for Geminis to switch careers in early middle life and chase success in a completely different direction. Again, the luck that seems to travel with those born under this Sign seems to protect them from the out and out disaster which often waits for others who attempt to change horses in midstream.

Those born under the Sign of Gemini can be quite ambitious. Often they are also original thinkers. With a new idea to pursue, Gemini is inclined to dash off without waiting to devise a strategy for success. Fortunately, Geminis not only love to make headway, but being adaptable and quick witted, they usually overcome their lack of planning. And with their fabled luck, they tend to crash through rather than simply crash.

Some Geminis have quite a flair for gardening and may, indeed, possess the proverbial green thumb. Some astrologers of old attributed the success of Gemini gardeners, born under the Sign of the Twins, to the Gemini ability to perform two tasks simultaneously, thereby achieving twice as much as gardeners born under other Signs of the Zodiac. The fixed star Aldebaran also affects those born under Gemini, and Aldebaran favors farming and agriculture.

Some Geminis may get themselves into strife with risky though exciting pastimes such as gambling. Double or nothing is often their motto. But knowing when to quit, either when ahead or behind, can be a problem for the optimistic and energetic Gemini.

A tenacious and patient business partner who revels in detail is a boon to Geminis who often flounder in it. Geminis usually need someone to follow through for them, to supply the practical back up necessary to implement their many bright ideas, the fallout from a typically Gemini brainstorm.

Love and friendship

Personally as well as professionally, Geminis tend to do well with partners who are more level headed, cautious and serious than themselves. Such partners complement the Gemini dynamo.

Even though Gemini men or women may be flamboyant to the point of being flirtatious, they demand unequivocal faithfulness from a partner and will be shattered by infidelity. They like their partner to be home oriented, even homely, just as they themselves rarely are. Often a Gemini person will find peace amid natural surroundings, gravitating to hobbies like recreational sailing, hiking or birdwatching, so partnership with another person who enjoys non-competitive outdoor pursuits is well augured.

On the negative side, Geminis can be irritating, especially when they're tired or frustrated. Their imaginative and impulsive natures may mean they try to do or think about too many things at once, making them quite exhausting companions. Don't expect a restful life if you are, or are close to, a Gemini!

Herbs and health

The planet Mercury is gardener to Gemini, providing herbs rich in minerals and organic salts to calm and soothe the sometimes frantic, quicksilver temperament of those born under this Sign. The herbs of Gemini include dill and caraway, parsley and lavender.

Prone to trying to do too many things at once, Geminis could find dill tea very calming. Caraway seeds and parsley, rich in iron and the A and C vitamins, are also good herbs for the Gemini.

Oil of lavender in a warm-water footbath will relieve the aching feet of Geminis who've overdone their natural inclination to swiftness and been on the run all day. A lavender-based facial sauna will help overloaded Geminis to establish their priorities. With a lavender-scented pillow or sleeping mask, Geminis experience deep relaxation — quickly! Speed is always of the essence to Geminis.

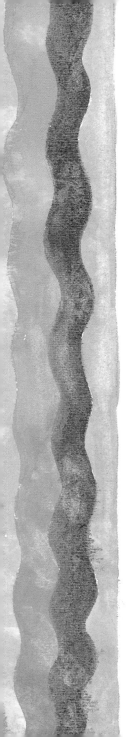

Cancer

22 JUNE — 22 JULY
PLANET — THE MOON
SIGN — THE CRAB
ELEMENT — WATER

Key characteristics

SENSITIVE, MOODY. QUITE AMBITIOUS. VERY PERSISTENT AND DETERMINED.

Temperament

Cancerians are among the lucky ones of life. They seem to be bestowed with health and stamina, personal beauty, charisma and original talents. This may be due to the influence in Cancer of the fixed star Alhena. Those professions which attract Cancerians are those which attract individualists who like to entertain, amuse, or in some creative way give pleasure to others. They are also renowned as extraordinarily hardworking people, naturally competitive, who deliver the goods. Though many are blessed with creative genius, the old saying that genius is one part inspiration and nine parts perspiration would strike a chord with most Cancerians. They find that they excel as tour guides, in public relations, sales, the travel and hospitality industries. Usually skilled public speakers, ambitious, responsible, methodical and sticklers for detail, Cancerians may reach the highest levels of government or community service. They often gravitate towards philanthropic work and have a strong sense of social justice.

Many Cancerians are so persistent that they prefer to see something through to the end rather than abandon it as a lost cause. 'Never say die' could well be the philosophy of this Sign. They can often withstand trials and tribulations which would destroy others. Given the fortuitous nature of the Sign, their setbacks often metamorphose into lucky breaks anyway!

23

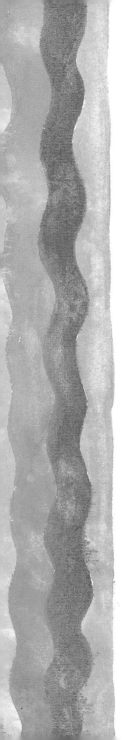

Emotionally, they share their namesake's thick, protective shell. Where others may lean on friends, partner or family under duress, those born under the Sign of the Crab are ultimately loners. This fortitude is also influenced by the fixed star Dirah, which bestows protection during hardship and adversity on those born under Cancer, especially those with birthdates between 22 June and 25 June.

The fixed star Pollux also throws its influence on Cancer. Pollux is the star of boxers and others who fight with their hands as weapons. Although they may first try to avoid a confrontation, Cancerians tend to be strong, aggressive fighters, willing to raise those 'claws' and fight fiercely for survival.

Born under the Sign of the Crab, hard outside and soft inside, Cancerians understand that looks can be deceiving and their intuition serves them well. They are ethical people, so Cancerian detectives with their instincts for subterfuge, sharp eye for detail, and powers of deduction are the ones to have on the hardest cases. Those born towards the middle of the Sign, around 29 June to 30 June, often have the gift of dreaming prophetically and of intuitive understanding. Many Cancerians are found among those celebrated as psychics and hypnotherapists.

Cancerians can be baffling to others. One minute they're full of confidence and enthusiasm; the next they've stopped in their tracks, on full alert, observing, assessing, reviewing, their entire being emitting an invisible but unmistakable 'Do not disturb' signal.

Sensitive Cancerians often are very fond of animals and may have quite a menagerie of pets. Farming sheep, cattle, pigs or poultry are some rural pursuits that may appeal to people born under this Sign. They also may be interested in or proficient at training animals such as dogs, horses or even lions!

On the downside, Cancerians can be so sensitive that it's difficult to speak to them without giving offense. Because they are such softies inside, despite their tough exterior and antennae for detecting enemies, many an empathetic or sympathetic Cancerian has been taken advantage of.

Responsible, commercially canny Cancerians are contradictory creatures in yet another way: they often handle money strangely. In a vivid and imaginative mood, they'll spend too freely, but overnight may become downright miserly. These swings can be unnerving for business or life partners pushed to see the Cancerian method in such apparent madness.

Love and friendship

Those born under Cancer should seek artistic and original-thinking partners, fond of company and travelling, for they do need stimulating companions although they are often very private people who need partners who also value a secure home life as much as Cancer does. Someone with a well-honed sense of the ridiculous, of the comic, will cope best and even enjoy the wonderfully contradictory elements of their Cancerian partner's personality and behavior.

Cancerians will only form partnerships after careful consideration, usually alone and without discussion. The oft-noted Cancerian moodiness will come into play, with Cancerians appearing quite withdrawn and taciturn as they debate any dilemma entirely within. Once they have made the decision to commit, they are usually loyal, even-tempered partners, personally and professionally. Happy and fulfilled Cancerians love to give enjoyment to their partners, and will often make a special fuss on birthdays and other anniversaries.

Cancerians value their individuality and if this is threatened, quickly retreat from relationships. At some point in their lives, Cancerians are likely to value independence and personal freedom above monetary gain or other people's opinions of them.

Herbs and health

Cancerians can be such introspective worriers that they develop stomach or liver disorders. Eyes, so important to observant Cancerians, must also be given special attention. Cancerians should look to herbs ruled by the Moon to suit the water element in their nature. Healing herbs for Cancerians are lettuce, agrimony, balm, chamomile and cucumber.

Cancerians who lie awake worrying at night would do well to have a bedtime cup of lettuce tea, an effective home remedy for sleeplessness.

Chamomile and cucumber will help clear blemishes and one of the oldest known remedies for easing tension around the eyes is to rest with sliced cucumber over each closed eyelid. Cancerians whose eyes are sore with strain will find it works like a dream.

Leo

23 JULY — 22 AUGUST
PLANET — THE SUN
SIGN — THE LION
ELEMENT — FIRE

Key characteristics

BORN LEADERS; LOVE TO MANAGE PEOPLE AND THINGS; VERY GOOD AT
SEEING THE 'BIG PICTURE.'

*The Lyon's herte is called of some men, the Royall Starre, for they that are
borne under it, are thought to have a royall nativitie.*
Wyllyam Salysbury, 1552

Temperament

Leos are usually very clever, imaginative, strong and resourceful people. Farsighted and
efficient, Leos work methodically towards a bright future, meeting difficulties with a
cheerful and warm countenance, creating opportunities out of obstacles. Leos have a
generosity of spirit which adorns any high-profile calling. They handle heavy responsibili-
ties with ease, are excellent at managing large-scale projects and expenditure. They
often shine as entrepreneurs, picking trends before others do, pioneering the way in
various fields of endeavor. The printing and newspaper industries are clear favorites with
Leos as are catering, entertainment, public administration
and politics. Leos may also be talent scouts, innovative builders or
architects, or expert in new product development. Because they love
to explore new territory and experience change, theirs is usually

27

an interesting and full life. Those born around 2 August are very fond of anything extraordinary.

Perhaps because they are highly imaginative, infectiously energetic and blessed with unflagging enthusiasm, Leos usually relate well to children. They're wonderful storytellers and great fun at parties.

One characteristic which they share with many children is a tendency to be contemptuous of authority for its own sake. They are equally dismissive of public opinion and likely to form independent and discerning views in which they grant no mercy to the bogus or undeserving. But to put it plainly, Leos should keep their thoughts to themselves once in a while. They can be overly fond of giving unsolicited advice. Their tendency to spout opinions can strike others as arrogant rather than forthright. Not everyone thinks the same way as the strongminded Leo and their views may needlessly offend others in certain circumstances. Young Leos starting out in the professional world should exercise caution when dealing with their superiors. In business, cultivating tact and the ability to keep silent when agreement is unlikely are desirable traits to learn.

Leos generally, especially those born from 26 July to 28 July, and no matter how outstanding their managerial talents, should be careful to mind their own business and not interfere in the affairs of others. Instead, Leos should channel their excess energies into public service, charitable works, or social groups where their infinite capacities for leadership, responsibility and management will be welcomed as committed and positive, rather than rejected as interfering and presumptuous.

The major Leonine weakness is vanity. It fools them into believing that they are supermen and women who can do everything — instead of supermen and women who can do almost everything. And it's a terrible thing to see a Leo come unstuck in the face of reality. The blow to their pride is a truly painful experience for them.

Love and friendship

People born under Leo need partners who though quiet themselves, will not be intimidated by any loud roaring or posturing! They should be able to maintain independent interests and opinions while providing

support and sympathy for busy, demanding, outgoing Leos. If it is a business relationship, Leo's partner should be the one good at accountancy and keeping records, with Leo front-of-house as sales or spokesperson for the partnership. Whether it is a personal or profes-sional relationship, their partners may be called upon to demonstrate manual dexterity because Leos are notoriously clumsy.

Leos also do well to temper their magnificent and independent personalities with a touch of humility. Without it, they can all too easily convince themselves and others that they need nobody except their own superior selves. And then they wonder why they share no deep and meaningful personal relationships! Why, Leos wonder, are they surrounded (at a safe distance!) by a circle of mere admirers?

Herbs and health

Leos are vital and fiery people. Physically, intellectually and emotionally, they are coura-geous and passionate, truly lion-hearted. Yet it is just these traits which may take their toll on Leos. Their healing herbs include borage, bay and saffron.

Borage with its star-shaped blue flowers, described through the ages as the herb of gladness, has long been used as a medicine for heart and circulatory disorders. Today's Leos, particularly those on healthy-heart, low-salt diets, will find its leaves an excellent salt substitute.

Early physicians also referred to the herbal pharmacoepia in conjunction with the Zodiac chart to prescribe oil of bay, extracted from the leaves of the European laurel, to relieve the arterial conditions which may afflict Leos. Crumbling a bayleaf or two into steaming vegetables or simmering hotpots is a healthy habit for Leos to acquire.

Fiery, golden saffron is appropriately ruled by the Sun in Leo. Those born under this Sign are well advised to seek out recipes using this precious ingredient. It turns bread-rolls, buns and rice dishes into golden meals fit for a king — meals that will help Leos keep fit, too.

Virgo

23 AUGUST — 22 SEPTEMBER
PLANET — MERCURY
SIGN — THE VIRGIN
ELEMENT — EARTH

Key characteristics

PERFECTIONISTS; HARDWORKING, METHODICAL, METICULOUS AND DETAIL ORIENTED. TRANQUIL, KIND, GENTLE, PEACE-LOVING.

Temperament

The Virgoan urge to create perfection reflects the innate creativity of people born under this Sign, their keen sense of aesthetics and order, and their natural predilection for the worthwhile in life. From a very early age they are often interested in the visual and decorative arts and crafts, antiques and fine music.

Their perfectionism also underlies their methodical approach to work, their gift for detail and accuracy. They tend to have quite exceptional memories and do well in tests involving mental calculation or factual recall. They usually make good students, historians, navigators and health practitioners. They are also keen and shrewd and these plus their other natural talents stand them in good stead if they follow careers in journalism — often indicated for those born towards the beginning of the Sign, from 23 August to 26 August.

The Virgoan's methodical nature also favors work which involves planning and periodical checking. They are happy to accept responsibility so careers requiring assiduous supervision and inspection such as editing, pharmacy, banking, insurance, and product management are indicated for Virgoans.

31

They are renowned for creating tranquil conditions about themselves, whether at work or at home. Virgoans often gravitate towards work linked with peacemaking and humanitarian issues, acting as go-betweens, arbitrators, diplomats, even missionaries. However, Virgoans typically work very hard, so that while working for the betterment of others they may simultaneously overlook their own wellbeing.

In those Virgoans born on 27 August, this capacity for hard work can co-exist with a quirky, imaginative element. These are the Virgoans who are likely to come up with a marvellous and challenging idea and then methodically complete each task necessary to launch it. Of all the birth dates in the Zodiac, this one nearly always produces an extremely interesting temperament. It is the birthday of the person most likely to invent something or suddenly demonstrate a previously hidden talent.

Virgoans born towards the middle of the Sign, from around 30 August to 5 September often possess psychic powers. These may manifest as a distinct occult ability or a discerning talent for readily assessing both the best and the worst characteristics of other people. Virgoans are generally kind natured, gentle folk, so their ability to detect undesirable acquaintances — and to guard tactfully against their advances — is a useful one.

Those born towards the end of the Sign, from around 9 September onwards, can be quite complicated individuals, combining a quixotic nature and a hasty temper with the more typical Virgoan eye for detail and highly retentive memory. They tend to be very lucky because this latter part of the Sign comes under the influence of the fixed star Zosma which brings benefits through the oddest and most unlikely situations. Sudden changes in fortune are the special hallmark of Virgoans born on or near 9 September. The downside for these Virgoans is that they seem to move through many relationships, both business and personal, because their nature is restless and they seek and attract change. They would do well to combine these traits with their methodical, meticulous Virgoan streak, finding the right occupational niche for themselves.

Love and friendship

Virgoans thrive in relationships when their partners unfailingly demonstrate total faith in the Virgoans' professional abilities. Those born under this Sign are well matched also with jolly, happy-go-lucky partners who can encourage them to relax, to remember that their love of perfection includes a love of peace and balance and a need for these in their own lives that they would be foolish to deny, to pace themselves if they are to achieve their major life goals. Learning how to play, to rediscover the joy and spontaneity of childhood is of vital importance to Virgoans for their tendency to work far too hard means that they may turn even their hobbies into work!

Kindly, protective, capable partners are ideal supports for Virgoans who typically are not particularly strong and can often overtax themselves. When stressed in any way, the Virgoan tendency towards being impossibly finicky and fussy, intolerant and critical of anything less then perfection often becomes more marked. Partners who can help Virgoans to keep their stress levels manageable are a boon to the partnership.

Virgoans are also inclined to get quite caught up with their own ambitions, so much so that they can appear to neglect family and friends while working themselves to exhaustion, becoming depressed and discouraged in the process. Virgoans will be well complemented by emotionally secure partners who will not feel hurt or abandoned when their Virgoans focus almost obsessively on work and career matters. Virgoans do need human companionship — they just may not be as demonstrative as some of the other, more fiery Signs!

Herbs and health

Virgoans, perfectionists that they are, set very high standards for themselves, then worry that they're not good enough to meet them! Theirs is a fragile self-confidence which means that many Virgoans, so placid and calm on the surface, may be inwardly seething with nervousness.

Fragrant, yellow flowered fennel, that herb with the soft, feathery foliage which belies the distinctive, anise-like flavor of its white bulb, is particularly indicated for the faint-hearted. Roman gladiators sprinkled chopped fennel over their food to give them courage, so it is ideal for nervy Virgoans whose biggest battle each day may be with their own lack of self confidence.

Tea made from Valerian, whose name is derived from the Latin verb valere (to be healthy), will also settle the nerves of Virgo.

Libra

23 SEPTEMBER — 22 OCTOBER
PLANET — VENUS
SIGN — THE SCALES
ELEMENT — AIR

Key characteristics

THOUGHTFUL. FRIENDLY. TACTFUL, PREFERS A PEACEFUL ENVIRONMENT, NOT GOOD WITH CONFLICT.

Temperament

The Libran habit of always considering both sides of every question is usually matched by an even temper, sound common sense and practicality. Librans tend to take their time to acquire any information they need or to measure situations and people. They are usually able to detect all that is fake or worthless. In turn, they are trusted and respected by others who admire their patient behavior and well-considered opinions. But their abiding Libran desire to strike the right balance in life can mean that they tend at times to be uncertain individuals, ditherers or procrastinators.

Given that they are born under the Sign of the Scales, it is intriguing that quite a number of Librans, in a wide range of occupations, do work which involves weighing and measuring. Librans are often found working as gem merchants, detectives, scientific researchers, scholars, politicians, craftspeople, and producers of finely manufactured goods. One relatively unusual field of endeavor which might well attract Librans investigating career options is meteorology, in particular weather forecasting since this involves balanced analyses of data to formulate predictions.

Some Librans further educate themselves in their later years simply because their orderly, alert and inquisitive minds enjoy stimulus. Their preferred fields of study often tend to

be unorthodox. Herbalism, hypnotism — any subject which allows for inquiry or debate attracts older Librans.

More than most Signs of the Zodiac, it is the Libran who will demonstrate strength of will and endurance in the face of adversity. Faced with difficult conditions, the Libran response is to persist. They will take pleasure, satisfaction and encouragement from small achievements in the absence of large ones. Adversity, by and large, only makes Librans more determined, more eager and more efficient in the long run. For this reason, a Libran will tend to do well following rural pursuits either as a hobby or as an income-earning way of life. Also pointing Librans towards rural matters is the fixed star Seginus under which they are born. Seginus is the source of their ability to achieve indirect and cautious progress. 'Hastening slowly' is the catchcry of many farmers successful because they know to wait and watch Nature signal the right times to sow and reap, to monitor markets so that they can trade livestock to advantage. Poultry keeping, fine horticulture and the cultivation of novel or hard-to-grow plants are all activities which may appeal to rural-minded Librans.

Libran fortitude is mirrored in their physical capacity as well, most Librans being blessed with constitutions which can withstand great strain. In physical appearance, the Libran man will often be very handsome, the Libran woman a beauty. While material fortune does not always shine on this Sign, their personal attractiveness, usually bright personality and measured approach to life counter any deficit.

This personal attractiveness may be quite notable in those Librans born between 2 and 3 October. These birthdates come under the influence of the fixed star Caphir which can bestow on those born under it the gifts of prophecy and charisma. Such Librans can be quite devastatingly attractive and talented people who will be in demand in any career depending on widespread public appeal.

Love and friendship

Librans tend to have a reliable and faithful nature, making them excellent partners both personally and professionally. In fact, Librans rarely experience difficulties in attracting partners. Their ideal

36

partners will share a great many Libran interests in both work and play.

Librans like to share and are very generous by nature. For instance they are usually very happy to entertain large numbers of people at home. Many Librans are particularly good cooks and hosts, being resourceful and thorough when it comes to organizing functions and considering the needs of guests.

Librans are born friendly; they are not inclined to moodiness and are less likely than other Signs to suffer from violent likes or dislikes. They often excel at giving others a shoulder to cry on. They'll readily discuss and take a sincere interest in their friends' or partner's problems. Usually quick to grasp the facts of any matter, most Librans are pleased to apply their Libran skills at orderly mental analysis to think things through and sound judgement to help their friends. Their talent for friendship often means that they enjoy true friends from many walks of life — despite the fact that characteristically warm and easy going Librans generally are lacking in humor. Strange as it may seem, many Librans have little if any sense of the ridiculous, of slapstick comedy, of satire or parody.

Herbs and health

Being born under the sign of balance has its negative side. Librans can be their own worst enemy when they try to continually weigh up all the facts and go on and on with decision-making.

According to herbalist diagnosticians, this sometimes amusing, sometimes infuriating, sometimes disastrous trait is physically paralleled by the Libran tendency to disorders of the body's elimination system. Herbal properties and astrological lore support their claims. For instance, the herbs ruled by Venus in Libra are very often diuretic (promoting the body's release of waste fluids).

The dandelion, which herbalist Nicolas Culpeper named 'piss a bed,' is one of Nature's best diuretics. Coffee may be made from its ground and powdered roots. But best of all, the dandelion's golden flowers can be fermented into a wonderful wine.

An infusion of sweet violets, an old remedy for kidney or bladder pain — well-suited to the Libran who is out of balance, — has strong tonic, antiseptic and purgative qualities.

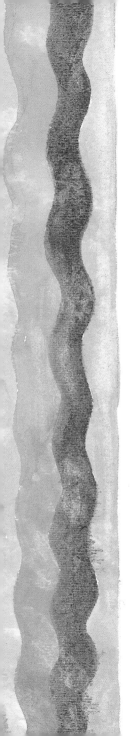

Scorpio

23 OCTOBER — 21 NOVEMBER
PLANET — MARS
SIGN — THE SCORPION
ELEMENT — WATER

Key characteristics

A BORN SURVIVOR. FREEDOM-LOVING. CONTRADICTORY, UNPREDICTABLE, VOLATILE.

> *... that cold animal*
> *Which with its tail doth smite amain the nations.*
> *Longfellow's translation of Dante's Purgatorio*

Temperament

While their passion for life makes Scorpios fascinating and disarming lovers, partners and friends, the sting in their tails is their love of freedom. Those born under the influence of Scorpio tend to chafe under any other influence. If not the maestro conducting the orchestra, then Scorpio is a soloist. Whatever their career choice, Scorpios are more inclined to excel when they're not tied to a team. But to maintain their motivation they must be sure their purpose is valuable, must have plenty of stimulus and variety in their work, and trusted support staff. Scorpio people should select business partners who are good planners and organizers, for while Scorpios hold the big picture in view with no trouble at all, they tend to ignore details, all of which Scorpio may regard as minor!

The Scorpios, true to their namesake's aptitude for survival, have a great knack for making the best out of unfortunate situations. When either outgoing and energetic or

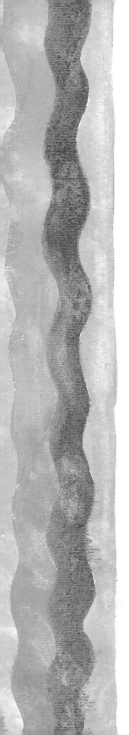

quietly but seriously committed to a project, Scorpio people are also more than likely to make good circumstances even better, often to the point of excellence. In their business and professional lives, they are shrewd and observant with a keen eye for new trends and unexplored opportunities, profitable alternatives and by-ways, by-products and spin-offs.

Whether predominantly introverts or extroverts, and Scorpios can be either, they generally look at life as an exciting adventure and seek stimulus from many sources. So theirs is often a complex and demanding program, with Scorpio playing a (major!) role in each of the many component parts of their lives.

The fixed star Alphecca in Scorpio particularly influences those born on 4 November. This is the birthdate of a truly powerful personality, perhaps someone who pursues a career which entails public performance or presentation. Alphecca is the star which brings happiness in love and worldly success to the horoscope, complementing the tenacious, forceful and ambitious nature of the typical Scorpio.

Scorpios born in the middle of the Sign, between 31 October and 2 November, are blessed with a fertile imagination which fuels their quite extraordinary talents for organization on the large scale. They may demonstrate a creativity directed towards being both pleasing and valuable to others.

All Scorpios can be impulsive and surprising, a direct result of the effect of the fixed star Princeps which creates all that is changeable and quixotic in their Sign. It is Princeps which inspires the Scorpion pioneering spirit and love of travel, prompts that part of them which is eager and impatient, restless and excitable, the volcanic interior concealed by their secretive, reserved and dignified facade.

They are sensualists who revel in food, wine, art and music, perfumes and fine linens. All are expert at finding a dozen little ways in which to indulge themselves everyday, sometimes secretly. They can become greedy materialists but on a higher level, this characteristic is expressed as a voracious hunger for knowledge, leading them to devour books or complete courses of study in record time. Often they combine pleasure with the generous and philanthropic side of their natures. Then they can work together with others, no trouble at all, finding pleasure in a good cause.

Love and friendship

Life is interesting for the partner of a Scorpio! One of their basic inclinations is to suspect others of wishing to control them. Patient indeed must be the one who loves a Scorpio. They're often very free with wildly exaggerated opinions and prepared to argue.

They can hurt their friends and lovers quite badly, for they have the meanest temper of all the Signs, theirs being governed by the fixed star Khambalia. In those Scorpios born towards the beginning of the Sign, its influence is slighter and their temper controlled to a dry-ice chill that burns. On those born on or around 29 October, Khambalia's influence is strong and they can be savage. Yet Scorpios are also tender-hearted and when remorseful will go to great lengths to make amends. For the typical Scorpio is more than a creature with a sting in the tail. The passionate nature of Scorpio shines through in their positive characteristics as well as in their less appealing ones.

Herbs and Health

The Scorpio person usually has great physical stamina which can come into conflict with the very capacity for survival from which it springs when Scorpios misuse it to push themselves too hard, too fast and too far. And just as they are contradictory and secretive people, so their stamina may belie some internal weakness. Many naturopaths believe Scorpios are particularly vulnerable to complications of the circulatory, reproductive and urinary organs.

The common stinging nettle may be just what the herbalist ordered for the creature who carries a sting in its tail to ward off harm. The juice of this readily available herb is said to be helpful with the high blood pressure which may trouble those born under Scorpio.

Tarragon and basil are herbs ruled by Mars in Scorpio. Hardy and ground-loving like the Scorpion, tarragon is found travelling over the hottest, rockiest patch of earth. Basil disappears in late summer, gone long before the first frost. Both herbs are ideal for flavoring the low-fat meals recommended on the healthy diets Scorpios love to hate. Firstly, freedom-loving Scorpio resents restrictions (which mean no secret chocolates!). Secondly, according to Scorpion taste buds, healthy food is bland beyond Scorpion endurance. Defy their dogmatic pronouncements: serve them a salad tossed with fresh young basil leaves or a tarragon flavored dressing. No typically sensualist Scorpio can resist.

Sagittarius

22 NOVEMBER — 21 DECEMBER
PLANET — JUPITER
SIGN — THE ARCHER
ELEMENT — FIRE

Key characteristics

IDEALISTIC, FREE-THINKING INDIVIDUAL. OFTEN VERY LUCKY, PARTICULARLY
IN TERMS OF MATERIAL WEALTH.

> *... glorious in his Cretian Bow,*
> *Centaur follows with an aiming Eye,*
> *His Bow full drawn and ready to let fly.*
>
> Creech's Manilius

Temperament

Sagittarians are invariably lucky: they're the success stories of the stock market, the ones who've made money by dealing in real estate. They have a definite knack for being in the right place at the right time. Lady Luck is their frequent companion throughout their lives.

But smiling Lady Luck's goodwill is rarely enough in life. Sagittarians certainly don't rely on it. Rather they attract more good fortune through their undeniable capacity for hard work. Moreover, Sagittarians possess a fine instinct for opportunity, a talent they appreciate and rely on increasingly as they progress through life and experience teaches them the enormous value of this talent.

Those born under the Sign of Sagittarius are generally personable and likeable people. They enjoy significant personal power both socially and professionally simply by being

themselves. In particular, those born on or around 6 December, are downright charming: bright, cheerful, chatty and enthusiastic about everything life has to offer. All Sagittarians are typically loyal, fearless, farsighted and often blessed with remarkably fine judgement (although they may be a little hot-headed or impulsive at times). These characteristics all hark back to their namesake, the Archer.

And like the mythical Archer, they are also strong individuals in their own right. They rarely lean upon others and usually think carefully before making a major decision or embarking on any significant activity. (They can deliberate for years before committing themselves to a personal life partner!)

But they are very action-oriented rather than passive people. Sagittarians are often those who initiate or generate response in others. As adults, they often demonstrate considerable talent as speakers, perhaps teachers, lecturers or trainers. They tend to gravitate towards occupations that allow for plenty of dynamism and movement, both physically and intellectually. Sales, travel, and the armed services are all likely to appeal to them.

Of all the Signs, they tend to have the greatest regard for human rights and the goodness inherent in humanity. This may lead them to work to improve peace and understanding at either a community or world level. Theirs is a world view, one which welcomes anything different, particularly foreign, and they are natural travellers.

Love and friendship

It may seem something of a contradiction then that the Sagittarian is the person most able and most likely to live alone. As a rule they have extremely high personal, moral and ethical standards, demanding the same high standards of others as they do of themselves. This profoundly important aspect of their nature leads them to be unsparing in their judgement of others and very sparing of forgiveness. Sagittarians are not likely to forgive and less likely to forget once they find someone guilty of transgressing the bounds of decent, civilized behavior in their dealings with the Sagittarian or with others, particularly the Sagittarian's family or friends. Not that Sagittarians are inclined to enjoy a quarrel or to smoulder as a Scorpio might. It is just that, once distrust and disappointment in the ethics of others has entered the Sagittarian mind, it tends to push aside any other bonds be those famil-

ial, social or professional. In the case of the Sagittarian born on or near 1 December, a time in the Zodiacal calendar which is directly affected by the fixed and fiery star Antares, any such falling out may be marked by drastic action on their part. An angry impulse on the part of a fired-up Sagittarian with a 1 December birthdate might result in a argument culminating with communications being permanently severed. With most other Sagittarians, however, such a break would be equally irrevocable but civil to a degree well below freezing point.

These high standards of theirs are another reason why Sagittarians tend to progress rapidly up the corporate ladder, or through the ranks of the army or navy. Their honorable character and clear convictions as to what is and is not acceptable behavior attract unswerving loyalty from others.

In addition to sharing the Sagittarian's high ethical standards, their ideal partner should be affable and easygoing, someone who won't want to share the Sagittarian's limelight, who won't be in any way a competitor for the admiration which the admirable and even quite dazzlingly attractive Sagittarian is used to receiving from the rest of the world. It will help if their partners are good communicators, intelligent and articulate people who will enjoy discussing the matters of worldly import and particular interest to the Sagittarian. Many Sagittarians will be more than delighted if their partner is simply an ideal listener.

Herbs and health

The active Sagittarian may well be one of those people who in later life suffers from rheumatism, particularly in the hips and thighs, the point of balance for the legendary Archer and the source of the muscular energy which releases the arrow from the bow with such force.

Nicolas Culpeper, the famous herbalist and astrologer of old, claimed that sage, being ruled by Jupiter, was an appropriate herb for Sagittarians. Cuts of meat to be roasted may be rubbed with sage leaves and sage tea is claimed to successfully darken greying hair.

In old herbal lore the leaves of chervil were said to be helpful to Sagittarians suffering from rheumatism and an infusion of chervil was recommended for people suffering from fever. By increasing perspiration, the infusion was said to help reduce body temperature — a boon for those with hot tempers from this fiery Sign!

Capricorn

22 DECEMBER — 21 JANUARY
PLANET — SATURN
SIGN — THE GOAT
ELEMENT — EARTH

Key characteristics

A STICKLER FOR JUSTICE AND DOING THE RIGHT THING. DETERMINED
PERSONALITY. HARDWORKING, DILIGENT, ENJOYS ROUTINE AND DETAIL.

> *Whoso is borne in Capricorn schal be ryche and wel lufyd.*
> *Natal Almanac, 1386*

Temperament

The Capricornians are the triers of this world, whether their skipping and leaping over and around the obstacles in their way or just plain stubbornly clambering up the slope of life! Determination and a will to progress onwards and upwards are hallmarks of this Sign. Hard work is no deterrent to a Capricornian. Their natural industriousness means that they invariably prefer the path of steady advancement. Get-rich-quick schemes have no appeal for them. They would prefer to be sure of arrival by travelling the longer but safe road than by taking a possibly risky shortcut. They are diligent workers to the extent that often even a very small Capricornian child will have an exceptional ability compared with other children of the same age to focus on a special project. Tending to be disciplined, methodical and careful in all undertakings, they show considerable talent in accountancy, finance and banking, as police, and in any mechanical trades.

Those Capricornians born in the second half of the Sign, from 3 to 5 January, usually have well developed artistic talents. These particular days also come under the auspices of

the fixed star Vega, which bestows a quality of personal magnetism and charisma.

Those Capricornians born towards the beginning of the Sign, on or around 24 or 25 December, are often good at coming up with fresh solutions to old problems. More usually however, Capricornians will be the ideal ones to inherit or absorb an idea from someone or somewhere else.

Capricornians tend to lack self-confidence and to be nervous. But these aspects of their disposition do not prevent them from speaking up for themselves or from trying to do their best, come what may. They are courageous people, pouring their enormous will to succeed into any worthy challenge.

They are modestly ambitious, pursuing achievement for practical reasons, rather than for power or control. In the business world, it is often the honorable Capricornian temperament that fuels their ambition and progress. For instance, they would be the first to become so disillusioned with what's wrong in their workplace that they would go about setting matters right, and without a thought to career consequences, earn themselves an enviable reputation and promotion in the process.

Capricornian diligence also tends to create Capricornian good fortune. Their industry is invariably rewarded with flourishing or expanding business. Large and extended families are also typically Capricornian! They are very productive people, in all senses of the word. Several marriages are often indicated in their horoscopes, too.

Of all the Signs, Capricornians have the fiercest sense of justice, adamant to say the least when compared to the calmer, even-handed Librans. They simply cannot stand back and observe unfairness of any sort but will do their level best to correct matters.

Nor do they reserve for others their critical and judgemental capacity. They apply the same strict sense of what is right and what is wrong, particularly what is fair and what is unfair, to their own motives and behavior and are notoriously hard on themselves — often far harder than they are on others.

Capricornians will never be candidates for abiding spiritual tranquillity. They are cursed, in a sense, with a nature which strives ceaselessly while always applying the highest standards equally to means as to ends. It is ironic that Capricorns who so often are found working for peace through political justice or to correct social injustices through philanthropic ventures, are unlikely to enjoy peace within themselves.

Love and friendship

Capricornians are warm and hearty people to whom others find it easy to relate. Their steadfastness and goodheartedness make them attractive as friends and partners.

Capricornians should seek a partner, notwithstanding their conviction that they can go it alone. The right partner is sometimes the only constant source of peaceful renewal for chronically strife-torn Capricornians, They really can do with someone to encourage them when life seems too much of an uphill battle, be supportive when they rage against injustice. They also should seek partners who have an aggressive edge to their personality, who accommodate change easily rather than treat it as an enemy, can confidently counter Capricornian caution when necessary and will not be bluffed or intimidated by a Capricornian in a goatishly forthright and self-willed mood!

Herbs and health

Determined they may be, but Capricornians are no strangers to depression. Even for them, there are times in life when obstacles seem insurmountable. They often need a little help to shrug off debilitating thoughts of defeat.

Furthermore, as they go about their daily lives, working hard and well, entering the lists to fight the good fight, courageous Capricornians seem to acquire more than their fair share of physical knocks and bumps.

Old herbal lore recognized these Capricornian propensities, too, maintaining that Capricornians tended to be downhearted at times and to suffer from knee pain and injuries, and to incur minor wounds and abrasions.

Comfrey — or knitbone as it was known in earlier days — has been prescribed for many years by herbalists to mend fractures, ease joint and muscle pain, and heal wounds. An infusion of comfrey is a soothing remedy for chapped hands.

An old European medicinal plant typically administered as tea to Capricornians who

were feeling low was the herb fumitory. Otherwise known as Bleeding Heart, it's name may ring a bell with many Capricornians. That's what they're called by those less idealistic and far more cynical than a true Capricornian could ever be!

Aquarius

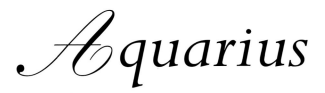

22 JANUARY — 20 FEBRUARY
PLANET — SATURN
SIGN — THE WATER BEARER
ELEMENT — AIR

Key characteristics

INDEPENDENT AND FIRMLY OPINIONATED. ATTRACTED TO SCIENCE AND THE ARTS. OCCASIONALLY ECCENTRIC, INCLINED TO PROCRASTINATE.

The sun his locks beneath Aquarius tempers,
And now the nights draw near to half the day,
What time the hoar frost copies on the ground
The outward semblance of her sister white,
But little lasts the temper of her pen.
Longfellow's translation of Dante's Inferno

Temperament

Those born under the Sign of Aquarius are valiant and self-confident people yet blessed by the absence of arrogance. They are unlikely to know defeat, certainly not permanently. Rarely can they be kept down for long by depression or adversity. In early life they may experience considerable obstacles but with time their way becomes easier and they eventually know the success they both seek and deserve.

Typically, an Aquarian is an adventurer but not foolhardy, tending to carefully assess situations in every aspect and keen to avoid exceeding their personal limitations, either financial, physical or psychological. While eager to discover fresh pastures, they are also reliable and can cope with emergencies and remain quite calm.

They are hard-working in their professional life and, without being fickle, may experience more than their share of job and career changes. This may be particularly so during middle life, when a whole new avenue may appear, offering potential success and headway in a completely different direction from that taken to date. Another typical development sees an Aquarian becoming involved in more than one business venture at a time. This situation may grow naturally from semi-professional hobbies, for instance, or may be deliberately sought by an Aquarian who wishes to take on more work to create more personal and financial profit in their lives.

Aquarians often demonstrate the enviable gift of being able to express a very creative mind via exceptional manual dexterity. Many embark on successful careers in which they continually explore these talents and skills. Those born under Aquarius are also those most likely to be blessed with an excellent financial sense so that they have an enormous range of choice across the entire spectrum of professions relying on financial skills.

Aquarians are quite unlikely to be spoiled by material success. They are blessed with a temperament which enjoy whatever it is they have and count their blessings. Greed and power-lust are not usually in their character. Often in later life, Aquarians turn towards work associated with improving the welfare of others, possibly using their innate powers of communication, often well-honed in their early to mid-life careers.

Aquarians are an interesting emotional mixture. On the one hand, their watery element can mean that they're not just super-sensitive, but over sensitive, inclined to respond with excessive or inappropriate emotion on occasions. However, Aquarius also frequently bestows the intangible and invaluable gift of intuition, specifically linked to the Aquarian ability to anticipate or tune in to other people's thoughts and feelings. Those Aquarians born on or around 27 January are the most sensitive of all. They may have to be scooped from the safe pond or backwater in which they will have immersed themselves for protection if they are ever to come into contact with the harsher world beyond. Further into the Sign, especially on or around 2 February, Aquarians will be gifted with a psychic power which will emerge in its own time.

Love and friendship

Aquarians are usually popular, the archetypal good friend and all-rounder. In turn, Aquarians enjoy people individually or en masse.

Indeed the Aquarian view of the world is truly global and one of their characteristic interests is in mass opinion and concerted, perhaps historical action. In their daily lives, Aquarians invariably demonstrate an ability to win the trust and friendship of very difficult people, such as very old or crotchety relatives, or a downright eccentric and idiosyncratic business contact. Their personal style, usually quite distinctive yet simultaneously very pleasing to many people is a simple manifestation of the personal magnetism which they enjoy. Those born on 6 February can be especially dazzling, with a sparkling mentality and an appealing, cheerful nature. This means that although they appreciate the input other people can provide in both a personal and professional sense, they tend to tackle all activities single-handed.

Ideally, Aquarians should seek partners who can exert restraint without either driving them to rebellious excess or suppressing their love of adventure. It is important that the partner have a spirit of adventure and a zest for living because a too-timorous attitude will only irritate headstrong Aquarians and possibly spur them into action they may not have otherwise taken. Aquarians will enjoy a companion who is quick-minded and versatile, commonsensical and very handy at organizing situations (usually when it comes to following through the Aquarian's initiatives!), very supportive and unlikely to oppose the Aquarian's projects. While Aquarians are not moody as a rule, those born on or near 29 January can be secretive. They, in particular, will be happiest with a partner who is cheerful and unconditionally affectionate.

Aquarians should, in short, choose friends and business associates with care, for their sensitive natures will always expose them to the influence of others, perhaps in quite subtle but nevertheless significant ways.

Herbs and health

Herbalists have long known that an infusion of elder flowers taken last thing at night soothes the spirit of a ruffled Aquarian who is suffering from nervous tension and who is unable to sleep. In winter time, warmed elderberry wine served with a little freshly grated ginger will do the trick.

Barley, ruled by the Aquarian planet Saturn, is generally beneficial for those born under the Sign of Aquarius. It is rich in magnesium, making it an excellent nerve tonic. Barley water, a famous old warm-weather drink, is generally nourishing and cooling.

Pisces

21 FEBRUARY — 20 MARCH
PLANET — JUPITER
SIGN — THE FISH
ELEMENT — WATER

Key characteristics

MARITIME INTERESTS PREVAIL. GOES WITH THE FLOW. USUALLY LOVES TO TRAVEL.

> *And here fantastic fishes duskly float,*
> *Using the calm for waters, while their fires*
> *Throb out quick rhythms along the shallow air.*
> Elizabeth Barrett Browning's *A Drama of Exile*

Temperament

Rather like their namesake, the Fish, Pisceans are seemingly contradictory in many ways. For instance, they will swim with the tide of life, going where it takes them, on course for many days, weeks, years at a time. Suddenly they're darting hither and thither, quite frenzedly and frequently changing direction, their former rhythm and routine abandoned apparently on a spur-of-the-moment whim and with the greatest of ease.

But this is the view of the outsider. For Pisceans are rarely, in fact, just going with the flow. They may look dreamily decorative, but do not be deceived. There's always a lot happening in the world of a Pisces. Fishlike, they are constantly receiving, processing and responding to a mass of environmental stimuli. Intelligent and sensitive for the most part, Pisceans pick up a lot more messages from the world around them than others realize.

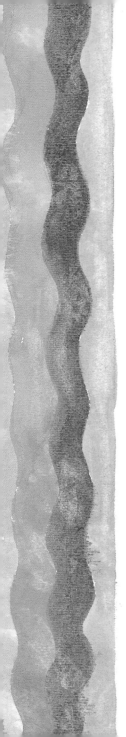

Subconsciously as well as consciously they sort this mass of information, a process which for them involves partial or at times complete withdrawal to some interior space impenetrable to others. They may appear smug, complacent or anti-social to the world when instead they are in a state of judicious detachment. Similarly, those sudden flicker-of-an-instant moves are simply the Pisceans in motion.

They are generally diligent people who enjoy quietly applying themselves to any sort of work where thoroughness, accuracy, a fine eye for detail and reliability count, including good planning and organizational skills.

Sometimes Pisceans gravitate towards a business opportunity which involves integrating art into the commodities of everyday life. Graphic design, fashion or furniture design, interior decorating or architecture are where such Pisceans might be found. They might choose to put their ability to process a great deal of detailed information to advantage in many fields. Horticulture, cartography and publishing are just a few.

They have a great love of learning and often demonstrate a quite remarkable capacity for storing and using knowledge. Librarianship is an obvious career choice but in more commercial enterprises it is the Piscean who can take on far more specialized work than, say, the Arian who is more inclined to entrepreneurial activities.

Those Pisceans born on 29 February in a Leap Year are usually very special people who combine the typically Piscean intelligence and capacity for hard work with a most unusual flair for living. This Leap Day is the birthday of geniuses and highly individual thinkers, the person who is not easily swayed by other people or circumstances, who is never likely to be roped into doing anything they do not want to do!

Aquarians are smooth, practical and single-minded when it comes to achieving business goals and can often demonstrate quite remarkable abilities in the fields of arbitration and mediation. Those Pisceans born under the fixed star Achernar, which particularly affects those born on 5 March, can often rise to quite prominent heights in a politics or industry. As with all Pisceans, they would do well to cultivate the tact and diplomacy necessary at the highest level in both those fields of endeavor.

Like their namesake, although Pisceans have a basically placid and self-contained nature, they also possess a capacity for hairtrigger aggression. This tendency to lash out suddenly is the personal challenge many a Piscean needs to overcome. In many instances their aggression is prompted by their sense of territoriality and a need to assert their presence and authority within their domain. In others it's their characteristic self-absorption which limits their consideration and tolerance for the rights of others who cross their path in life.

The nice thing about Pisceans is that the baited hooks of personal power and material success are unlikely to have any attraction for them. They are quite unimpressed by glamour and have no desire to possess luxurious belongings or enjoy a millionaire's lifestyle.

So too are Pisceans generous with others in all sorts of ways. They rarely miss a chance to do a good turn. Medieval soothsayers used to counsel Pisceans, above all the other Signs in the Zodiac, to always help others, and turn a bad deed to a favor. The logic underlying this advice was that as fish living in a pond are part of a community in which individuals rely for survival on a common code of mutual respect and civilized interaction, so the greatest Piscean good fortune returns as a result of doing favors for others.

Love and friendship

The Piscean often can be quite suspicious of other people. However, once a friendship has been established, it is likely to be a lifelong and very deep one. Plenty of tolerance, cheerfulness and stability on the part of their partners will offset any temperamental Piscean temperamental whims or outbursts. If their partners are creative and imaginative, even poetic by inclination, so much the better, for the Pisceans are great romantics. Artistic or otherwise creative people are also more likely to understand the paradoxical Pisceans, in turn tranquil and hyperactive, gentle and aggressive, introverted and extroverted, self-centered and yet affectionate and generous.

Herbs and health

Pisceans need to beware of ailments linked with cold and damp. A very old remedy for warding off winter chills and colds which every Piscean should take note of is the bright

red rosehip which is rich in vitamins A and C. Lungwort, a member of the borage family, is a herb ruled by Jupiter in Pisces. As the name implies, country folk held it in great esteem for treating chestiness, coughs and sneezes.

$\mathscr{R}$ising Signs

A rising sign shows your public persona, the way you are with people who do not know you very well. It describes the part of you that is on display, at job interviews and parties for example; it is your social mask. This outer image may be quite different from your inner nature or true personality and knowing your rising sign will give you a further insight into yourself.

Look up your star sign in the chart opposite and then your time of birth. This gives you your rising sign.

RISING SIGNS

	2am	4am	6am	8am	10am	Noon	2pm	4pm	6pm	8pm	10pm	Midnight
Aries	Aquarius	Pisces	Aries	Taurus	Gemini	Cancer	Leo	Virgo	Libra	Scorpio	Sagittarius	Capricorn
Taurus	Pisces	Aries	Taurus	Gemini	Cancer	Leo	Virgo	Libra	Scorpio	Sagittarius	Capricorn	Aquarius
Gemini	Aries	Taurus	Gemini	Cancer	Leo	Virgo	Libra	Scorpio	Sagittarius	Capricorn	Aquarius	Pisces
Cancer	Taurus	Gemini	Cancer	Leo	Virgo	Libra	Scorpio	Sagittarius	Capricorn	Aquarius	Pisces	Aries
Leo	Gemini	Cancer	Leo	Virgo	Libra	Scorpio	Sagittarius	Capricorn	Aquarius	Pisces	Aries	Taurus
Virgo	Cancer	Leo	Virgo	Libra	Scorpio	Sagittarius	Capricorn	Aquarius	Pisces	Aries	Taurus	Gemini
Libra	Leo	Virgo	Libra	Scorpio	Sagittarius	Capricorn	Aquarius	Pisces	Aries	Taurus	Gemini	Cancer
Scorpio	Virgo	Libra	Scorpio	Sagittarius	Capricorn	Aquarius	Pisces	Aries	Taurus	Gemini	Cancer	Leo
Sagittarius	Libra	Scorpio	Sagittarius	Capricorn	Aquarius	Pisces	Aries	Taurus	Gemini	Cancer	Leo	Virgo
Capricorn	Scorpio	Sagittarius	Capricorn	Aquarius	Pisces	Aries	Taurus	Gemini	Cancer	Leo	Virgo	Libra
Aquarius	Sagittarius	Capricorn	Aquarius	Pisces	Aries	Taurus	Gemini	Cancer	Leo	Virgo	Libra	Scorpio
Pisces	Capricorn	Aquarius	Pisces	Aries	Taurus	Gemini	Cancer	Leo	Virgo	Libra	Scorpio	Sagittarius

Chinese Years

ACCORDING TO THE ancient Chinese system of astrology, your life and character are shaped by the particular year in which you were born, not by the days and months.

Under the Chinese astrological system, each year falls within one of the twelve heavenly constellations or Mansions. These are named for the characteristics they share with twelve of the creatures which roam the Earth below. The Twelve Animals by which the Chinese identify each of these Heavenly Mansions are the Dragon, Snake, Horse, Sheep or Goat, Monkey, Rooster, Dog, Boar, Rat, Buffalo or Ox, Tiger, and Rabbit or Hare.

As the planet Jupiter travels through its twelve-year circuits of the Sun, it passes through one of these twelve Mansions each year. Those born in that year, within the shelter of that Mansion, will share its characteristics and its fortunes.

Through centuries of studying these distinctive Mansions and their interaction, the Chinese have gradually and thoughtfully developed a series of notions which further symbolize the qualities and powers attributable to each year. These are as follows:

YEAR	MYSTIC SYMBOLISM
Dragon	Seedtime
Snake	Supremacy of yang
Horse	Yin reasserting itself
Sheep or Goat	Taste of fruit
Monkey	Yin going strong
Rooster	Completion
Dog	Exhaustion
Boar or Pig	Root in soil
Rat	Rebirth of vegetation
Buffalo or Ox	Hand half-opened
Tiger	Awakening of life
Rabbit or Hare	Plants emerging from the soil

So, to the astrologers of the ancient East, people are to be understood best as individuals who were born in a Year of the Dragon or a Year of the Snake, a Year of the Tiger or one of the Rabbit, a Year of the Rooster, Buffalo, Boar, Rat and so on.

Which are you? And what does life hold in store for you? Check the date of your birth against the list on the next page, then read on!

CHINESE TWELVE YEAR HOROSCOPE

YEAR OF THE DRAGON
1904 1916 1928 1940 1952 1964 1976 1988 2000

YEAR OF THE SNAKE
1905 1917 1929 1941 1953 1965 1977 1989 2001

YEAR OF THE HORSE
1906 1918 1930 1942 1954 1966 1978 1990 2002

YEAR OF THE SHEEP OR GOAT
1907 1919 1931 1943 1955 1967 1979 1991 2003

YEAR OF THE MONKEY
1908 1920 1932 1944 1956 1968 1980 1992 2004

YEAR OF THE ROOSTER
1909 1921 1933 1945 1957 1969 1981 1993 2005

YEAR OF THE DOG
1910 1922 1934 1946 1958 1970 1982 1994 2006

YEAR OF THE BOAR OR PIG
1911 1923 1935 1947 1959 1971 1983 1995 2007

YEAR OF THE RAT
1912 1924 1936 1948 1960 1972 1984 1996 2008

YEAR OF THE BUFFALO OR OX
1913 1925 1937 1949 1961 1973 1985 1997 2009

YEAR OF THE TIGER
1914 1926 1938 1950 1962 1974 1986 1998 2010

YEAR OF THE RABBIT OR HARE
1915 1927 1939 1951 1963 1975 1987 1999 2011

YEAR OF THE
Dragon (Long)

THE CHINESE DRAGON is a symbol of virtue and strength, not the gruesome monster of medieval European imagination. Trustworthy, courageous and fierce, Dragons guarded the treasure of the Chinese gods. Throughout Chinese history, the emperors were closely associated with the Dragon, theirs being the Dragon Throne. The Dragon is a mighty protector. It looks after those born to its House and is thought to roam beneath the surface of the earth, bringing woe to those who injure or offend its own.

Indeed Dragons rank with the other major Chinese symbols of good fortune: water and jade. If you were born in a Year of the Dragon then you will know health and happiness.

When considering their bodily health, those born in a Year of the Dragon should be particularly attentive to their ears. The Dragon is traditionally thought to be subject to hearing difficulties and therefore vulnerable to enemies.

The Dragon is also thought to confer the gifts of natural vigor and sexual potency on those born under its dominion. Those born in a Year of the Dragon are smouldering, passionate and extremely attractive to others.

They should look for friends, lovers, business and personal life partners among those born in the Years of the Tiger, Rooster, or Rat. With these people in their lives, success will come more quickly and happiness will be experienced more intensely by those born in a Year of the Dragon.

One flaw of many people born in the Dragon's Mansion is impulsiveness. They can also be quick tempered and stubborn. Those born in a Year of the Dragon will never let anyone push them around!

They are usually very lucky in terms of material wealth. Just as well, because those born children of the Dragon are much inclined to favor the luxurious and the expensive things in life. Dragon extravagance is legendary: when feasting on oysters nourished by the friendly element of water, they would spit out the pearls for the use of those born to their House. Those born under the influence of the Dragon often have some special connection with water in their lives.

YEAR OF THE
Snake (She)

IF YOU WERE born in a Year of the Snake, a Chinese astrologer would expect you to be charming and clever, gifted with the supernatural powers attributed to reptiles. Ancient Chinese believed that if you were a Snake person, you could transform yourself into a fairy, demon or elf at will, just as a snake can shed one skin for another.

But a Chinese astrologer would also know to expect that there is more to someone born within the Mansion of the Serpent than may ever meet the eye. With those born in such years, what you see is often not all you get! These people can be still waters running deep, keeping their true thoughts and feelings to themselves. At best, they place a high value on privacy as distinct from secrecy. At worst, they are capable of duplicity and perfidy, with the potential to develop awesome powers of cunning for evil purpose. Treacherous people are described by the Chinese as 'snake hearted.'

If you were born under the influence of the Snake perhaps you're already notorious for smooth-talking your way out of tricky situations, wriggling out of things you don't want to do, perhaps stretching the truth ever so slightly as you make excuses?

But then people born within the House of the Snake are almost irresistible. The result is that others tend to flatter and fuss over them to such an extent that those ruled by the Snake may become vain and selfish. Even so it is hard to not to like them! They have tremendous personal magnetism and are usually very attractive to others. Although all may not be as slinky as they would like, those with the Snake as their emblem are usually very sexy people! As partners, they should avoid people born in the Years of the Tiger, the Boar, or the Rooster who could bring them bad luck. Instead, they should seek friends and lovers among those born in Years of the Buffalo or the Monkey.

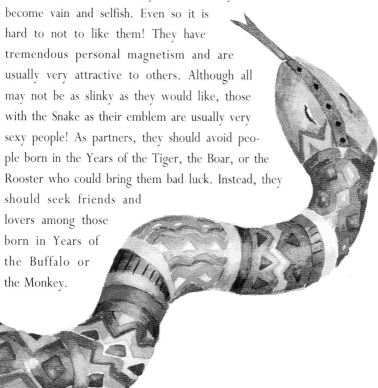

YEAR OF THE
Horse (Ma)

CHINESE ASTROLOGY HOLDS that those born in a Year of the Horse are likely to enjoy high status, be very influential in some way, and to experience material affluence in their lives. In ancient China, horses were symbols of high rank, great power and wealth, reserved for the sole pleasure of the nobility, for hunting and for warfare.

The qualities of endurance and courage for which horses are renowned are also found in those born in a Year of the Horse. Soldiers born in those Years were highly valued in the great cavalry and infantry battalions assembled by the legendary Chinese warlords.

Horses in the wild are very active and intelligent animals, benignly noble creatures, beautiful in their finely-tuned senses and their ability to outrun their natural enemies. So, too, are those born in a year of the Horse. They prefer to be always doing something, constantly on the go. Many are extremely talented at whatever they choose to do and will go a long way in life, easily outstripping the competition. But they're also

inclined to be temperamental, impatient and a little intolerant of those who cannot keep pace with them! The many gifts of those who live within the Heavenly Mansion of the Horse come with the responsibility to fulfil their human potential with humility.

Those born within the astrological Mansion of the Horse are usually considered lucky. Chinese folklore has it that the presence of those born in a Year of the Horse protected livestock against theft, disease and harm from evil spirits.

And just as horses are naturally trusting, affectionate and sociable animals, if you were born in a Year of the Horse you should always be on your guard against your own inclination to gullibility in personal relationships. Those who bear the emblem of the Horse are far too inclined to fall in love too often, too easily, not wisely but too well! If only you would be more careful and select your lovers from those born in the Years of the Tiger, Goat or Dog!

Sheep or Goat (Yang)

WITHIN CHINESE CULTURE, the sheep is the symbol of modest devotion to family, always depicted kneeling respectfully to either give or receive nourishment. So if you are born within the House of the Sheep then you will be highly valued by your family for your quiet commitment to them all.

Sheep-people are regarded as amongst the luckiest of all. It is thought that those born within the protection of the Sheep will never experience hunger. Such people were those whom the Chinese assigned to take charge of farming during times of drought and famine, for they were thought to have a lucky effect on the cultivation of the soil. And those born in a Year of the Sheep are usually very lucky with money.

Not so with romantic love. Perhaps this is because those born under this Sign are notoriously self-effacing. Then, too, those born with the Sheep as their life symbol can be far too inclined to take things slowly. If you're a sheep, you'll not be one of those who marry in haste and repent at leisure.

The prospect of anything new or strange tends to frighten you: new faces, new places, the never-ending changes in our world. And you often approach anything different with trepidation, fearing the worst.

In fact, your big weakness may well be pessimism. Too often those born under the influence of the Sheep are inclined to look on the black side, worry about things which may never happen, see difficulties which simply do not exist. If you're born with the Sheep as your personal emblem, then you need a partner who is optimistic and brave — and who can cope with you when you get in one of your fearful 'down' moods! You are most likely to find one of these paragons in those born when Jupiter is in the Mansion of the Boar, the Horse or the Rabbit.

YEAR OF THE
Monkey (Hou)

THE MONKEY IS a highly prized animal to the Chinese. At one time, only members of the Imperial family were allowed to keep them as pets. Being born in a Year of the Monkey was thought to ensure an advance in status within your lifetime.

If you were born in the Year of the Monkey, then you may well be very clever, perhaps a genius. Yours is a highly passionate nature. For instance, you adore sex and you also avidly pursue money and success. But although very passionate, most people born in the Mansion of the Monkey are very clearheaded about what they want out of life and generally succeed in getting it without too much difficulty. But they can be difficult to get along with at times, just like their fascinating animal namesake. Being unpredictable and changeable is, of course, part of your charm for others if you were born in a Year of the Monkey. But these same qualities can also be very irritating to others at times. More so when as a Monkey-person you get a bit obsessed with getting what you want, now! At such times the flash of the Monkey symbol is enough to make anyone dive for cover, for then those born to that Heavenly House may be selfish and quarrelsome to get their own way.

As partners, those born in a Year of the Snake will appreciate your sexiness (you two would make a very hot little number indeed!) and be more than your equal in charm and cleverness. Those wearing the emblem of the

Rat will adore your changeability while instinctively knowing where to draw the line with your demanding Monkey-type mischief.

Monkey people, perhaps because they can be such mischiefs themselves, were believed to have the power to drive evil spirits away from themselves and others close to them, and by controlling witches, elves and hobgoblins could bring health, wealth and success to others. So while they may be a bit of a trial at times, Monkey people have a lot to offer their partners!

YEAR OF THE
Rooster (Ji)

THE ROOSTER IS very potent symbol amongst the Chinese people, signifying the Sun and therefore the fiery concept of Yang which is masculine and active.

Above all, those born into the Heavenly House of the Rooster are said to have the power to bestow good or inflict evil upon their fellow men and women. In earlier days, an individual born in a Year of the Rooster would be invited into the homes of other Chinese people in order to frighten away evil spirits. Such an individual's name, together with a picture of a rooster, would be pasted onto a barn as a protection against fire.

If you are born under the influence of the Rooster, you have many good qualities. Like your namesake, you are extremely self-confident, physically strong, brave in body and spirit, and always active, punctual and reliable. Your word is your bond. Your are outstanding in your capacity for developing and sustaining the highest level of self-motivation, for taking the initiative, and for very hard work of any kind.

Your wonderfully passionate nature may, however, sometimes lead you astray. You can, in fact, be a bit of a hothead when it comes to lovers. For instance, you often find yourself madly attracted to a person who turns out to be one to hurt your feelings badly. Others may try to warn you that you're headed for yet another heartbreaking disaster, but stopping a Rooster person in full romantic flight is no job for mere mortals. You stand a better chance of happiness in personal relationships if you seek to find a partner among those born in either a Year of the Dragon or of the Buffalo.

When things do work out well for you on any front, then the whole world knows it. As a Rooster, you know that you're just sharing the good news of your success, just being your naturally exuberant self. Unfortunately, to the rest of us sometimes it sounds just like good old-fashioned crowing!

YEAR OF THE
Dog (Gou)

IF YOUR HEAVENLY House is shared with the Dog, you are one of those fortunate few in life who, even in this materialistic age, do not hanker after money or possessions. What really matters to you is freedom to do and say what you like. You will go your own way in life, untroubled by conventions and speak out loudly for what you regard as your own rights or those of others.

One of the nicest aspects of those born within a Year of the Dog is their honesty and fidelity. Many centuries ago, the Chinese writer Khan Hsiang-tao wrote of those born in a Year of the Dog as follows:

The Dog is a man who keeps watch, is skillful in his selection of other men, and will keep away from anyone who is not what he should be.

Those with the Dog as their emblem are indeed very likely to be blessed with a high intelligence combined with an even temperament and pleasant disposition. They dislike hasty decisions, preferring to chew things over. In that way, they're a bit like a dog with a bone! And they can be stubborn at times, particularly when it comes to admitting they might be in the wrong.

They also love their creature comforts: a warm bed, a favorite chair, sitting by an open fire in winter, catching the cool breeze from an open window in summer.

No doubt their honest, generous natures, together with their love of home comforts spawned the old Chinese tradition of asking those born under the influence of the Dog to bring good fortune to homes and villages by staying overnight.

But everyone has enemies at times and if your Chinese astrological Mansion is that of the Dog then you may strike some bad days with those born in Years of the Dragon, Rooster or Rat. But you will also find yourself with staunch allies, a blessing due in no small part to your own gift for loyalty to others inspiring great loyalty to you. Look for such friends among those born in the Years of the Tiger, Rabbit and Horse.

YEAR OF THE
Boar or Pig (Zhu)

BEING BORN IN the Year of the Boar means that you enjoy the good life, and plenty of it. Gourmet food, expensive clothes, jewellery and elegant surroundings are very important to you. So much so that you may be none too fussy or considerate of others when it comes to how you go about making sure such pleasures are part of your life. An old Chinese proverb reads:

The coming of one born in the Year of the Boar into the House betokens poverty while the advent of one born in the Year of the Dog riches.

The notion is that one born to wear the emblem of the Boar will eat you out of house and home while a person true to the House of Dog is a giver not a taker.

Not that those born in the year of the Boar are dishonest. Far from it. You're quite open about what you want out of life. Intelligent and hard-working, too. Although when you do end one of your marathon working sessions, you know how to relax!

Your undisguised materialistic values, your single-mindedness in pursuit of your goals, and prolonged periods of deep respite can convince others that you are shallow , greedy and lazy. With such an astrological reputation preceding you, it's no wonder that those born within the influence of the Boar cannot expect to have too many friends through life. But Boar people, at their intelligent bon vivant best, can be wonderful friends, savagely loyal and protective too. So though they may have few friends, those will be loyal for life, happy to overlook any boorish behavior. These friends are likely to be born in a Year of the Rabbit or the Goat. The natural enemy of boars and pigs are snakes, so steer clear of those born in a Year of the Snake.

YEAR OF THE
Rat (Shu)

ACCORDING TO CHINESE mythology, the Rat is blessed with long life and supernatural powers. People who are born in the Year of the Rat are often described by the Chinese as having 'an old soul' and for many centuries Rat people were thought to be most likely to bear messages from the transmigrated souls of relatives and friends.

They are thus considered to be among the lucky ones of this world: clever and fortunate throughout their long and happy lives. They attract good luck as honeypots attract bees. Moreover, your luck spills over from your own life into that of others who quickly perceive that it's great having you around. For many centuries in China, people believed that those born in the Mansion of the Rat were empowered to grant or deny good fortune to others. Accordingly, those born in a Year of the Rat were treated with enormous respect and showered with gifts. But be careful: your popularity could be your undoing. Whatever you do, do not let other people set the agenda so that you find yourself organizing or restricting your own life to suit theirs.

Those wearing the emblem of the Rat must be true to its incorruptible and independent spirit and travel their own way in life. When necessary to avoid the demands of others, you could take advantage of the cunning, crafty and secretive elements of your nature. But you must watch that those traits do not become flaws in your ambitious, hardworking character.

Also, you should watch your temper. Born under the influence of the Rat, you can turn suddenly angry, perhaps be quite vicious. This may happen when easygoing, companionable you lets yourself get caught up in other people's lives at the expense of your own work or play. Just like a Chinese firecracker you explode in all directions, shooting off sparks of frustration and thwarted independence. No wonder your family and friends describe you as being 'a bit ratty' at times!

For a harmonious life with considerate partners, choose those born in Years of the Monkey, Buffalo or Dragon and do your polite best to avoid those born in the Year of the Goat or the Horse.

Buffalo or Ox (Niu)

IF YOU WERE born in the Year of the Buffalo, you are fortunate, attracting good luck towards both yourself and those close to you. An old Chinese proverb says of those born in the Year of the Buffalo:

They will repress the evil spirits that disturb the lakes, rivers and seas.

The Buffalo is emblematic of spring and agriculture, so those born under this Sign are particularly associated with bringing good fortune to new beginnings and ventures on land. It is also traditionally reminiscent of peasant toil in the fields of China, so Buffalo people are usually thought to be hardworking, humble in nature. No one should be surprised if they become involved with agricultural pursuits.

It may seem strange to Westerners that the essentially feminine yin principle is represented by the symbol of the Buffalo, surely one of nature's creatures most renowned for size and strength. Conversely, Chinese culture regards the Buffalo as an animal close to the soil, to Mother Earth. That's why Chinese astrologers expect females born within the Heavenly Mansion of the Buffalo to be the most feminine of people, their instincts for nurturing developed to the highest level. Similarly, men born under to this House are blessed with the gift of understanding women as few born to other Houses can. Never will you see a man born with the Buffalo as his emblem saying to a woman: 'But I've no idea what I've done to upset you!' or 'What are you so upset about?' To boot, they're usually a handsome lot, tending to be the strong, silent, passionate sort.

Both sexes born within the Buffalo's Heavenly Mansion are clever, imaginative, intuitive, patient and understanding. However, they have two major faults they should guard against: they tend to keep themselves too much to themselves, and they are sometimes too stubborn. They do best with partners born in a Year of the Snake, Rooster or Rat.

YEAR OF THE
Tiger (Hu)

THOSE BORN UNDER the influence of the Tiger, are considered to have enormous talents for making money and every likelihood of material success. The Chinese Malay God of Wealth is sometimes portrayed mounted upon a tiger.

Tigers have long been an emblem of bravery and ferocity. If others come under their protection, then those people will have every cause to feel safe from other earthly predators. As the poet William Blake said:

> *Tiger, tiger burning bright ....*
> *Did he who made the Lamb, make thee?*

Those born under this Sign often strike other people as far too intense, dynamite in fact. Then on days when Tiger people are presenting a cool front they can be easily misunderstood as uppity, standoffish and unfriendly.

Either way, others learn quickly to approach Tiger people with caution. The usually magnificently handsome men and women born as children to the Tiger are not only dominating but highly critical of those who can't match their stern intelligence or explosive energy.

Courageous and adventurous, if you are born in the Heavenly House of the Tiger, then you revel in risk as others do in a warm bath. Chinese gambling dens use tigers as a symbol to advertise their establishments. Highflyers and hard players, rebellious to all authority if they're in the mood, people born in a Year of the Tiger love to live life right 'on the edge.' If you are one, be warned: even those with their namesake's feline grace and sure-footed sense of balance must stumble at times.

If you are born to the Heavenly Mansion of the Tiger, there will be days when you'll find you agree with those who believe that life is not meant to be easy. In fact, you are often unlucky in love. Lucky at cards, unlucky at love as the saying goes.

Tiger people will have better luck in life as well as in love if they can manage to fall for partners born in a Year of the Dragon, the Dog and the Horse. They should be wary of adding to their bad luck in every way if they form liaisons with anyone born in the Years of the Monkey or the Snake.

YEAR OF THE

Rabbit or Hare (Tu)

GOOD LUCK AND bad luck will be yours in life in roughly equal proportions if you were born in the Year of the Rabbit. You may be aware of this already, for Chinese astrologers also attribute to you the ability to foresee the future!

The Rabbit is said to be a supernatural creature of auspicious omen whose fate is traditionally associated with the Moon. Chinese astrologers pay great attention to the position of the Moon when preparing the personal horoscope of one born in the Mansion of the Rabbit. Buddhist legend tells that Buddha rewarded a rabbit's extraordinary courage and fidelity with reincarnation as the Man in the Moon. Other folklore tells that in ancient China, an Imperial officer stole the elixir of life and fled with it to the Moon where as a white hare he sits beneath a cassia tree to pound with mortar and pestle the ingredients of immortality.

If not immortality, then certainly longevity is thought to characterize those born beneath the influence of the Rabbit. One Chinese legend tells of a rabbit who lived one thousand years, turning white only when it reached the five hundred mark!

If you are born within a Year of the Rabbit, usually you will be lucky in a material sense, being adept at making money and advancing quickly in your career largely as a consequence of your own talents and efforts. You are clever and imaginative, hardworking and resilient, able to keep going at a project when others want to call it a day.

You are also very articulate and have a distinct ability to smooth out difficulties which may arise with colleagues or relatives. But your love life is not so easily fixed. Nearly all Rabbit people suffer broken hearts at some time or other. Try to avoid this by bestowing your affections on someone born in a Year of the Boar, Dog or Goat. Jade, symbolizing longevity and good fortune, is said to be an especially lucky gem for those born within a Year of the Rabbit.

Birth Flowers

JANUARY — CARNATION

Columbine,
With gillyflowers,
Bring coronation and sops in wine,
Worn of paramours ...

Edmund Spenser

To those born in January, the well-loved carnation promises a life of variety and empowers them with the quality of courage.

FEBRUARY — VIOLET

Violets dim,
But sweeter than the lids of Juno's eyes
Or Cythera's breath

As a birth flower, the violet symbolizes the gentle qualities of modesty and shyness together with strength of character in adversity.

March —
Daffodil

For oft, when on my couch I lie
In vacant or in pensive mood,
They flash upon that inward eye
Which is the bliss of solitude
And then my heart with pleasure fills,
And dances with the daffodils.
William Wordsworth, Daffodils

The spiritually uplifting daffodil bestows dignity and chivalry on those born in March, the
earliest month of the northern hemisphere's springtime in
which it first blooms.

April —
Sweet pea

Here are sweet peas, on tiptoe for a flight;
With wings of gentle flush o'er gentle white,
And taper fingers catching at all things,
To bind them all about with tiny rings.
Keats, I Stood Tiptoe Upon a Little Hill

Together with grace and a sense of delicacy, the sweet pea
brings with it the possibility of a varied life for the versatile
April-born.

MAY — LILY OF THE VALLEY

That shy plant ... the lily of the vale
That loves the ground, and from the sun
withholds her pensive beauty.

Wordsworth, *The Excursion*

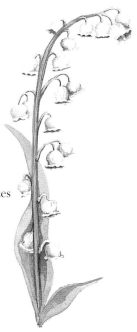

Liliy of the Valley is a very auspicious birth flower. It symbolizes happiness, joy, optimism and bright new beginnings throughout life.

JUNE — ROSE

What is more tranquil than a
musk rose blowing
In a green island, far fro all
men's knowing?

John Keats

Love is the magnificent birth gift of the rose, some representing aspects of love — rosebuds signifying unawakened love and yellow roses jealousy.

July — Larkspur or Delphinium

Named for the irrepressible dolphin (from the Greek delphis), the blooming delphinium bestows health and a talent for happiness on those born in July.

August — Poppy

If ye break faith with us who die
We will not sleep, though poppies grow
In Flanders' fields ...

John McCrae

The poppy's many blessings are a capacity for renewal, an understanding that there's a time for every purpose: beauty, grief, loyalty and courage.

SEPTEMBER — ASTER

The scarlet of the maples
can shake me like a cry
Of bugles going by.
And my lonely spirit thrills
To see the frosty asters like
a smoke upon the hills.

Bliss Carman, A Vagabond Song

Grace, modesty and a sweet of disposition are bestowed on those given the stylish aster which is considered emblematic of elegance, friendship and secret love.

OCTOBER — CALENDULA OR MARIGOLD

The marigold that goes to bed
with the sun,
and with him rises, weeping.

Shakespeare

Those born with Marigold, follower of the sun, as their mistress are spirited lovers of nature, radiating happiness to all around them.

NOVEMBER — CHRYSANTHEMUM

The chrysanthemum symbolizes perfection which is often expressed as the well-balanced philosophies of life practiced by those who call it their birth flower.

DECEMBER — HOLLY

That in my age as cheerful I might be
As the green winter of the Holly Tree.

Robert Southey, The Holly Tree

Holly, emblematic of physical and spiritual renewal, bestows the gifts of foresight, strength and resilience on those who are born in December.

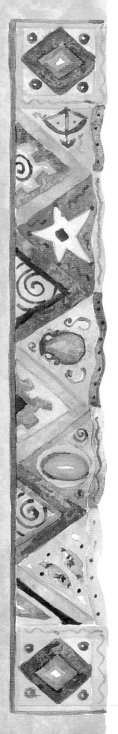

Birth Stones

ARIES

THE DIAMOND IS the emblem of fearlessness and invincibility, a fine choice for self-expressive, enterprising, impatient Aries. It was thought to bring victory to those who wore it by endowing them with extraordinary courage and strength. The dazzle and flash of the diamond was said to manifest its wearer's capacity for awesome and unconquerable energy. An ancient poem offers this salute to the diamond:

> *The Evil Eye shall have no power to harm*
> *Him that shall wear the diamond as a charm.*
> *No monarch shall attempt to thwart his will*
> *An e'en the gods his wishes shall fulfil.*

The diamond has also inspired much folklore. It is variously reported to protect against poison, as a baffle to black magic, to dispel vanity and fear, and to bring success in lawsuits. Cypriot fishermen believed a flashing diamond attracted schools of fish. The ancients claimed that if you swallowed a diamond, you would never have a sore throat. Cleopatra used her diamonds to inspire her lovers.

TAURUS

21 APRIL — 20 MAY
GEMSTONE — EMERALD

THE EMERALD WAS much used in divining future events and to reveal the truth in any situation. No wonder then that this gemstone is in astrological harmony with the typically straightforward, truth-loving Taureans.

Long regarded as aids to Venus and Cupid, emeralds were used to determine the truth of a lover's oaths. One ancient piece of advice recommends that a husband who fears he is being cuckolded, conceal an emerald in his wife's food who would be unable to swallow the green gemstone of truth if guilty. It's hard to imagine swallowing an emerald without noticing! One can only hope that not too many faithful wives who coughed up emeralds weren't cruelly tested in this way, with insult added to injury when their fiendish husbands (doubtless emerald green with jealousy) accused them of infidelity.

Emeralds were much used in healing: Aristotle claimed that wearing an emerald about the neck (so important to Taurus) prevented fits. Emeralds were believed to bring other benefits to their owners, too, like making them smarter, richer, and more eloquent.

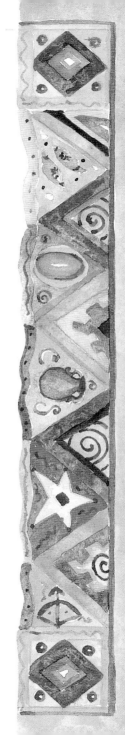

GEMINI

21 MAY — 21 JUNE
GEMSTONE — MOONSTONE

THE GENERALLY SENSITIVE, complex, faithful and romantic Gemini people are truly represented by these translucent gems, from white to palest pink, distinguished by a characteristic bluish sheen, delicate and mysterious.

The moonstone is found mainly in Sri Lanka (formerly known as Ceylon) where it is a sacred stone. Sri Lankan legend has it that the most beautiful moonstones are washed up by the tides every twenty-one years when the Sun and the Moon come into their most harmonious astrological conjunction. At such times the hem of the Moon's silvery robes, the waves of the sea, brushes the Earth's shores to reveal its treasury of moonstones.

The moonstone thus represents the wealth which flows from the harmony of two who are as one, the harmony of Gemini. Moonstones rank highly as gifts for lovers. It is said that if, under the light of a full Moon, two lovers hold the stone of faithful Gemini, they will foresee the future of their life together.

CANCER

22 JUNE — 22 JULY
GEMSTONE — CARNELIAN

CARNELIANS WERE ONCE called cornelians (derived from the Latin word for cherry) and its name is accurately descriptive of this gemstone which is usually a warm cherry red in color, as luscious to the eyes as the best cherries of summer are to the taste.

Carnelians actually range in color from bright red to a warm honey color. The bright red ones are said to appease anger while honey-colored carnelians are said to exhilarate the soul and banish fear. Just the gemstone for those born under the Sign of the Crab: sometimes cranky, sometimes fearful, always supersensitive softies inside their tough exteriors.

Along with the other reddish stones, carnelians are said to staunch bleeding and it was once thought to cure snakebite. The wearing of carnelians is also recommended for those with a weak voice or who are timid of speech, for the warm-colored carnelian is said to add timbre to vocal tones and give courage to nervous speakers.

An early Spanish ditty which sings the praises of the carnelian translates as follows:

Carnelian is a talisman
brings good luck to child and man.
If resting on an onyx ground
A sacred kiss imprint when found.
It drives away all evil things
To thee, and thine protection brings.

LEO

23 JULY — 22 AUGUST
GEMSTONE — SARDONYX

THE SARDONYX, SYMBOLIZING dignity, is highly compatible with the characteristically kingly instincts of those born under the Sign of the Lion.

In years gone by it was recommended as a shield against sorcery and harmful incantations and was believed to sharpen the wits of the wearer. The sardonyx, with its two, clearly marked, parallel bands and colors (deep red for loyalty and white for fidelity), visually symbolizes married bliss (in which typical Leos luxuriate). An anonymous poet of old advised husbands and wives:

> *Wear sardonyx, or for thee*
> *No conjugal felicity.*
> *The August-born without this stone*
> *'Tis said must live unloved, alone.*

One famous sardonyx was that given by England's Queen Elizabeth I to the Earl of Essex. The Queen commanded a lapidarist to carve the gemstone with her image and set it in gold as a ring for her favorite. When later imprisoned for treason, Essex sent this ring to Elizabeth as a reminder of their bond, with a letter of appeal for his life. But their enemies intervened: she did not receive the memento and Essex was beheaded. Elizabeth's grief for Essex is said to have contributed to her own death only weeks later.

VIRGO

23 AUGUST — 22 SEPTEMBER
GEMSTONE — SAPPHIRE

THE SAPPHIRE SYMBOLIZES nobility, virtue, justice, and loyalty, qualities in harmony with the Virgoan quest for perfection in themselves and others. According to Hebrew tradition, the Rod of Moses and the stone tablets bearing the Ten Commandments were set with sapphires. Roman Catholic cardinals receive sapphire rings when invested as Princes of the Church. And famously exquisite sapphires are found in many collections of royal or state jewellery.

The sapphire, it's said, attracts divine favor, protects its wearers from envy and against all harm. Virgoans who've been overdoing things, or worrying that they can't meet their own high standards, may be interested to learn that sapphires were also used to treat anguish or distress, as this old rhyme suggests:

A maiden born when autumn leaves
Are rustling in September's breeze,
A sapphire on her brow should bind
To cure diseases of the mind.

LIBRA

23 SEPTEMBER — 22 OCTOBER
GEMSTONE — OPAL

OPALS VARY WIDELY in popularity and acceptance. Opals are said to guard their wearers against lightning strikes and also thought to cheer the heart and mind. Some say this stone is unlucky, particularly for the eyes, a belief stemming from the mediaeval word 'ophal' or 'opthal' for the Evil Eye. Others claim opals protect the wearer's eyes because opals are so responsive to light. How typically Libran that these gems should attract quite varied and opposite views!

The ancient Roman naturalist Pliny the Elder certainly admired the opal — which was also his birthstone. His Libran love of beauty and of elements in harmony is expressed in his description of the opal:

It is made up of the glories of the most precious stones ... the gentler fire of the ruby, the brilliant purple of the amethyst, the sea green of the emerald, all shining together in incredible union.

SCORPIO

23 OCTOBER — 21 NOVEMBER
GEMSTONE — TOPAZ

THE YELLOW TOPAZ, from wheat to bronze in color, is the best known of these gems. But there is also a colorless or white topaz, plus red, pink, pale green and pale blue. Whatever their color, they symbolize cheerfulness, perhaps because of their astrological association with the life-giving Sun. Tradition holds that if topaz is to exert its full power, it's warm, light-filled, energetic vibrations should be complemented and reinforced by a gold setting.

Those wearing topaz are said to be able to ward off danger and to prevail against sorcery. Other claims for topaz include the power to cure nervous ailments, prevent nightmares, calm madness and violent passion, restore sight, and augment the wealth of its wearers. Heliodorus said that topaz made people invulnerable to flames and a Roman fable claims topaz can restore sight.

So who wouldn't feel cheerful wearing topaz? Certainly not typical Scorpios, dazzlingly powerful and passionate, keen to make the best of things, lovers of warmth and all creature comforts, delighting in variety. And a bit greedy, too, sometimes. They're bound to want a topaz in every color! And set in gold, thank you very much!

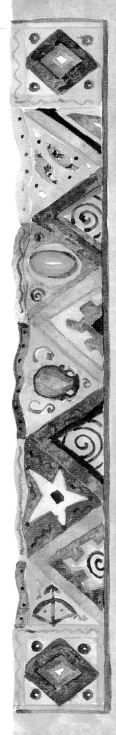

SAGITTARIUS

22 NOVEMBER — 21 DECEMBER
GEMSTONE — TURQUOISE

CHARMING TURQUOISE IS the symbol of luck and love. But perhaps you can only have both if you're a typical Sagittarian, notoriously lucky and likable, despite being simultaneously romantic, freedom-loving, and ethical.

Turquoise long ago acquired a reputation as a love charm. In Shakespeare's The Merchant of Venice, Leah gives a turquoise ring to Shylock to win his love.

Turquoise also has been assigned many protective powers down the centuries. Turkish cavalrymen used to attach the gems to the bridles of their mounts to prevent the horses from stumbling, themselves from falling, and injuries to men and beasts.

The turquoise is said to cheer the soul and strengthen the eyes of the wearer. It is also said to avert the Evil Eye, but if the color pales the wearer is in danger. Similarly, the turquoise was supposed to grow paler as wearers sickened and upon their death to lose color entirely:

> *The compassionate turquoise that doth tell*
> *By looking pale, its wearer is not well.*

CAPRICORN

22 DECEMBER — 21 JANUARY
GEMSTONE — GARNET

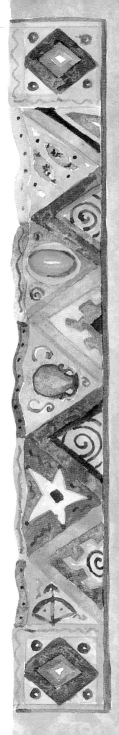

GARNETS COME IN various red shades, the deepest so dark it is near-black to the naked eye, the palest a transparent pink. Red-green garnets are rare and highly-prized. Emblematic of constancy and fidelity, the garnet is true, too, to the Capricorn instinct to be always rational yet faithful and devoted either to cause, religion, loved one or any focus of attention of their judicious minds and hearts.

Not surprisingly, garnets have an honorable and romantic reputation in legend and history. Noah's Ark was said to be illuminated by a finely chiselled garnet. The fourth Heaven of the Koran (the sacred scripture of Islam, believed by orthodox Muslims to contain revelations made by Allah to Mohammed) was said to be made of garnets. To honor his marriage and his new Queen, the British monarch, George III, presented his wedding guests with garnets set in gold and inscribed George and Charlotte united 1761.

Garnets were also believed to possess healing powers. The yellow variety was said to cure jaundice. Red gems were prescribed to relieve fever and depression. Medieval Christian Crusaders believed garnets afforded protection against wounds and other misfortunes.

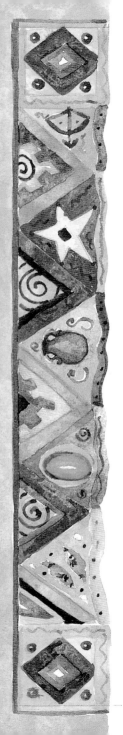

AQUARIUS

AMETHYSTS, SYMBOLIZING SOBRIETY and temperance, are highly compatible with the Aquarian temperament: friendly, popular, but also idealistic, self-reliant and reliable. The name comes from the Greek amethystos. Legend tells that Bacchus, the Roman god of wine and a lusty, drunken reveller occasionally, tried to seduce the virgin nymph Amethyst whom he loved but who did not love him. Desperate to protect her maidenhood, she appealed to Diana, goddess of chastity, who changed Amethyst into a pillar of white crystal. Driven by guilt about his behavior, remorse at its terrible consequences, and grief for his lost love, Bacchus poured over the pure white crystalline form of Amethyst his most exquisite wine, giving the gem its mauve to violet colors.

As a symbol of perfection, a famous statue of Apollo, the Roman god of masculine beauty, was given amethyst eyes. The Romans believed that an amethyst gift from a wife both flattered her husband and kept an otherwise wayward partner sober and true.

During Nero's reign, Romans arrived at orgies with amethyst ornamented goblets. Thus equipped, they felt free to enjoy themselves, confident that they'd never be so intoxicated that they'd miss a moment's fun.

PISCES

THE DELICATE AND translucent aquamarine is the symbol of elegance. The name aquamarine comes from a combination of the Latin words for water and sea, the natural elements of Pisceans. Folklore has it that the gem we know as aquamarine earned its name because its color compares with the blue-green color of Aegean sea water held momentarily in cupped hands, as elusive as any typical Piscean. According to Mediterranean myth, aquamarines were originally washed ashore from the jewel caskets of mermaid treasure deep in the sea. With a history rich in myth and mystery, the aquamarine is in absolute harmony with the typically enigmatic Piscean personality.

Pisceans are frequently renowned for their fine eyesight and for being both intuitive and perspicacious. In the Middle Ages, the Piscean birthstone was called 'the magic mirror,' many people then believing that those wearing these gems acquired the power to read the thoughts of others. The aquamarine was regarded as having medical and healing powers particularly in relation to the eyes — early German health practitioners prescribed grinding the stones for use in the lenses of spectacles to cure short-sightedness.

Colors

ARIES

21 MARCH — 20 APRIL
RULING PLANET — MARS
RULING COLOR — RED

RED CONTAINS ENERGY to equal the typically forceful temperament of those born under Aries. Those who subscribe to the healing power of color, use red to counter negative thinking and to improve vitality, especially in those with weak blood or poor circulation.

TAURUS

21 APRIL — 20 MAY
RULING PLANET — VENUS
RULING COLOR — PINK

PINK IS THE color of love. Rose pink symbolizes romantic love and encourages sympathetic feelings between people generally. Pink is the color most likely to reduce the effects of stress or create the 'rosy glow' we enjoy in positive and nurturing environments.

GEMINI

21 MAY — 21 JUNE
RULING PLANET — MERCURY
RULING COLOR — YELLOW

YELLOW REPRESENTS THE nervous system which it is said to stimulate and strengthen. A yellow room is a powerful environment in which to work or grow, so is an ideal choice for generally optimistic, energetic, versatile and creatively self-expressive Geminis.

CANCER

22 JUNE — 22 JULY
RULING PLANET — MOON
RULING COLOR — VIOLET

VIOLET IS THE MOST spiritual color in the spectrum, the one most likely to trigger mental relaxation and meditation, well-suited to the sensitive, persistent, deep thinking and introspective Cancerians. Its healing powers may benefit the entire nervous and cerebral system.

LEO

23 JULY — 22 AUGUST
RULING PLANET — SUN
RULING COLOR — ORANGE

WHAT OTHER COLOR could so well reflect the fiery and powerful Leo personality? Above all, it inspires achievement. It is most stimulating but not exhausting. Strong and rich, packed with positive vibrations, orange is a beneficial choice for big-hearted Leos.

VIRGO

23 AUGUST — 22 SEPTEMBER
RULING PLANET — MERCURY
RULING COLOR — BROWN

TYPICAL VIRGOAN, PEACELOVING, practical and hardworking, know the pleasures of a rich, warm brown, a color symbolic of the soil of planet Earth and promising good fortune through stability. Browns may be used to reassure and calm self-doubting or distressed Virgoans.

LIBRA

23 SEPTEMBER — 22 OCTOBER
RULING PLANET — VENUS
RULING COLOR — INDIGO

LIBRANS ARE GENERALLY friendly people, fond of harmony, so cool indigo blue of the gentle vibrations is their lucky color. The ancient Greeks believed indigo helped regenerate the brain, a notion echoed by New Age therapists who use dark blue to counter fear and frustration.

SCORPIO

23 OCTOBER — 21 NOVEMBER
RULING PLANET — MARS
RULING COLOR — BLACK

POWERFUL BLACK BRINGS luck to the strongly individual and independent Scorpio personality. Wearing black, they are being true to the Scorpion's secretive natures. In an assertive mood, they choose black with red. Black with blue counters their Scorpion tendency to tense introversion.

SAGITTARIUS

22 NOVEMBER — 21 DECEMBER
RULING PLANET — JUPITER
RULING COLOR — LIGHT BLUE

PALE BLUE, SYMBOLIZING clarity, enhances the powers of forward-looking Sagittarians. Wearing pale blue robes, the nine Muses of Greek mythology brought inspiration, the gift of the gods, to those mortals chosen to achieve immortality through artistic and scientific development.

CAPRICORN

22 DECEMBER — 21 JANUARY
RULING PLANET — SATURN
RULING COLOR — GREEN

COOL AND SOOTHING green is used in color therapy to heal and calm both mind and body. Its powers of balance and harmony simultaneously complement the systematic Capricornian approach to life and promote peace within for the restless, ever-striving Capricornians.

AQUARIUS

22 JANUARY — 20 FEBRUARY
RULING PLANET — SATURN
RULING COLOR — ROYAL BLUE

NATURALLY DIGNIFIED, ACTIVE, independent, thoughtful and creative Aquarians are well stimulated and complemented by the clear, tranquil and refreshing vibrations of royal blue. Color therapists use royal blue to help restore self-confidence and to increase levels of mental and physical energy.

PISCES

21 FEBRUARY — 20 MARCH
RULING PLANET — JUPITER
RULING COLOR — AQUAMARINE

THE FASCINATING AQUAMARINE, simultaneously blue, green and turquoise, both invites and defies definition, mirroring the typically changeable Piscean personality. The color of freedom, aquamarine brings luck to travellers, feelings of hope to those shackled or isolated by fear or confusion.

$\mathcal{N}$umbers

FOR CENTURIES, MYSTICS and philosophers, mathematicians and alchemists have experimented with numerical systems to explore the significance of numbers in our lives. For instance, not too many generations ago, it was said that one should never speak one's age aloud, for once in possession of those numbers, the ever-listening Forces of Darkness would have the power to cause great harm to one's body or soul. How much of that old belief lingers today in people's reluctance to reveal their age?

In more benign mood, a number cycle dating back to the days of the Ancient Greeks summarized human life in terms of seven-year stages:

- *the 1st seven years* — the teeth grow in
- *the 2nd seven years* — the ability to produce seed
- *the 3rd seven years* — the beard grows or womanhood develops
- *the 4th seven* — maximum strength is reached
- *the 5th seven* — the season for fruitfulness and marriage
- *the 6th seven* — the time when intelligence reaches its height
- *the 7th seven* (a very lucky time) — the maturity of reason
- *the 8th seven* — intelligence is perfected
- *the 9th seven* — we become gentle and mild
- *the 10th seven* — the end of life

Birth numbers or personal destiny numbers are easy to calculate. Discarding all zeros, you total your date, month and year of birth and reduce that figure to one digit. If your birthday was on the twentieth day of September, the ninth month of the year 1939, number 6 would be your personal destiny number:

$2 + 9 + 1 + 9 + 3 + 9 = 33 = 3 + 3 = 6$

Each primary number or birth number from 1 to 9 has a specific meaning and is governed by a planetary force:

1. Ruled by the Sun, this number, truly indivisible, signifies power, independence, responsibility and action. People with this birth number are leaders rather than followers, sometimes overbearing or intolerant.

2. This is the number ruled by the Moon, the planet which fosters harmony on the planet Earth by favoring love and union, diplomacy and tact, negotiation and settlement, and all cooperative ventures of genuinely mutual benefit to the participants.

3. A lucky number governed by the planet Jupiter which enhances individual optimism, sociability and creative self-expression. Conversely, Three may indicate procrastination, carelessness and extravagance.

4. This number is ruled by the planet Uranus which brings efficiency and practicality to those born under its influence. The negative possibilities of this number include prejudice and resentment.

5. Five, a quixotic number of quicksilver temperament and ruled by the changeable planet Mercury, is usually the birth number of a communicator or someone extremely creative and very possibly artistic.

6. Ruled by the planet Venus, this number promises fame and possibly the gift of prophecy to its sympathetic, loving children who may suffer from anxiety or a jealous temper.

7. A very lucky number under the influence of the planet Neptune. Fine powers of sympathy, intuition and second sight are in its giving, as are its negatives, moodiness and depression.

8. Eight, ruled by the sometimes ruthless planet of Saturn, is a symbol of survival, indicating an analytical, efficient and controlled personality, sometimes intolerant.

9. A multiple of lucky Three, so also a lucky number, is ruled by Mars, the planet of compassion and generosity on one hand, self-centeredness and emotional volatility on the other.